To Todd

KING

KELLY

COLEMAN

kentucky's greatest basketball legend

GARY P. WEST

STEWARD & WISE PUBLISHING
Morley, Missouri

STEWARD & WISE PUBLISHING
P.O. Box 238
Morley, MO 63767
(573) 262-3994

Consultant: Douglas W. Sikes

Book Design: Wil Sikes

Cover Design: Emily Sikes

Photos pages 104, 107, 108, 109, 110, 111, 112 and back cover
courtesy of the *Lexington Herald-Leader.*

Copyright © MMV

Library of Congress Control No.: 20059334771
ISBN:0-9773198-0-6

Second Printing: 2005 A.D.

Printed in the United States of America

10 9 8 7 6 5 4 3 2

Contents

*Dedicated to the coal town of
Wayland, Kentucky and all of the
other mountain communities with a
similar way of life.
It was these eastern Kentucky coal camps
that have added to the incredible legacy of
basketball throughout Kentucky.*

Foreword

There are any number of reasons why this story will appeal to readers. First, it is the titanic struggle of one man's attempt to overcome his surroundings by playing a game that is revered in his home state of Kentucky. Secondly, it is a portrayal of who is arguably the best high school player to have ever played the game of basketball in the Bluegrass, and finally it is the story about Kentuckians and their love affair with this wonderful game. By the time "King" Kelly Coleman finished his high school career at Wayland High School he was known throughout Kentucky and beyond its borders for his basketball exploits. He was a phenomenal scorer and rebounder and he did it all so effortlessly. While his performance on the court was on most nights, flawless, his private life bordered on tragic. His marriage, personal relationships, and life after basketball were filled with disappointments and failures mostly brought on by his battle with the bottle.

While Kentucky has produced a number of high quality basketball players in the decades it has been playing high school basketball, no one could invigorate or enliven a crowd or spark a debate about the finer points of the game than "King" Kelly. The way he shot the ball, the frequency with which he shot it, his uncanny knack of rebounding his own shots all generated conversation around those warm coal-burning stoves on those cold winter nights.

Often times I don't think athletes, particularly those in their late teens or early twenties, realize the influence they have on younger impressionable boys and girls. In one week in March 1956 one "King" Kelly Coleman put on a scoring exhibition in the state tournament that is still talked about today. In the crowd that week was a skinny 12-year-old with a close-cropped "flat top" and his best friend. If there was ever any doubt that youngster would end up playing the game of basketball, it was put to rest that week.

I was that 12-year-old. Thanks, Kelly.

Larry Conley

Larry Conley
University of Kentucky 1964-66

Introduction

Writing a book can be a daunting task. There are so many more people involved than first meets the eye. I've always heard that you really haven't lived unless you write a book or run for political office. Now I've done one of them. The other may come later.

I want to start by thanking my mom and dad for insisting that I stay in school and get my education. It was tempting along the way to become a statistical dropout, but they wouldn't let me.

Then there were the countless hours at the word processor by my wife, Deborah. They may have been countless to me, but I think she counted everyone of them. It was her encouragement, telling me how much she enjoyed what I was writing, that made it easier for me to write the next chapter.

Early on I knew she was into the book. When talking about Kelly Coleman, she always, and I mean always, refers to him as "King Kelly Coleman."

My thanks to Jerry Fultz and Patty Murphy at the Wayland Historical Society for opening up their files and gathering information. Jerry was like my left arm, always there. His enthusiasm and dedication to preserving the wonderful history of Wayland is contagious. He sure did make my life easier. Unfortunately Jerry's brother, Billy Ray Fultz, one of Kelly's teammates, died shortly after being interviewed for this book.

Doug Gott, a friend and sports junkie, put another set of eyes on the manuscript. His constructive suggestions were accepted, and because of that, this book is better.

There were all of Kelly's teammates along the way, high school, college and pros. There were opponents, men who had played against him. There were people who had only seen Kelly play. They didn't actually know him, but they had a story to tell.

There was ex-wife, Ann, who obviously logged many steps with Kelly as he plodded from one path to another in order to keep his basketball dream alive before settling down in Michigan.

Then, of course, there is Kelly. Without him there is no book. Even though we have become friends, I had to remain objective. But to Kelly's credit, that's the way he wanted it. He assured me from the outset that he wanted the book to be an accurate portrayal of his life. As long as it was the truth he was okay. I thank him for that.

Some eighty interviews and a year and a half later, I have a book.

Preface

never intended to write a book. When I met Kelly Coleman for the first time, my intentions were to interview him, find out what he's been doing all of these years, write a nice story, and then see if one of the area magazines might want to print it.

Obviously it became more than that.

In the beginning I wanted to write about a high school basketball legend from 50 years ago, who for some reason never became what some had expected of him.

I was 13-years-old and in the seventh grade the first time I heard the name King Kelly Coleman. Growing up in Elizabethtown, Kentucky, I lived a long way from the mountains of eastern Kentucky. It was another world. But even as a grade schooler I was one of those sports junkies. I couldn't get enough. Back then *Sport* magazine was the bible, not *Sports Illustrated.* I read the *Louisville Courier-Journal* in the morning and *The Louisville Times* in the afternoon. Sports writers Earl Ruby and Dean Eagle were who I read first. Their by-line meant you could believe it. Bob White and Earl Cox came a little later, but not much.

If they wrote about it, it must be important. And they began to write about Kelly Coleman back in 1956, as did sports writer Billy Thompson at the *Lexington Herald-Leader.*

When it came to Kelly Coleman, however, all of them, followed the lead of long time writer Gordon Moore who covered mountain basketball for some 30 years.

It was Moore who told the rest of the world that, indeed, there was a special basketball player in eastern Kentucky and his name was King Kelly.

Coleman disproved the old adage that people remember only the winner and never who came in second. During that 1956 High School State Tournament, Coleman and his Wayland teammates didn't even finish second. They finished third. But his scoring exploits, 50 years later, are remembered as much as the Carr Creek team that won it all.

From that time forward, King Kelly has been somewhat of a mystery.

Is he still alive?

Where did he end up playing?

What happened to him?

Where does he live?

Why doesn't anyone ever hear about him?

There is a mystique out there. One thing is for sure, he does not suffer from over exposure.

There have been stories written about Kelly Coleman. There have been writers who have tried to figure him out, to find out why he did what he did. But none of them ever started at the beginning. It seems like everything written about him revolved around that one single event in March of 1956 - - the Sweet 16.

Kelly's life is about much more than four basketball games. He had a life well before and long after those games in Lexington, and, with Kelly, in order to come even close to finding out what makes him who he is, you've got to start at the beginning.

KING
KELLY
COLEMAN

Chapter 1

Time has not yet robbed Wayland of its biggest claim to fame . . . home of King Kelly Coleman.

Wayland is a small coal town that appears to have seen its better days, a town that long ago has been passed up by time. Yet there are those who remain, making the best of it, even to the point of talking about a future.

Evidence of this can be found at the Historical Society/ Community Center, a modern building that is pretty much the hub of any activities that occur in the town. And right next door is Bobby Hamilton's Wayland Kwik Mart. Both of these entities pay homage to their most famous citizen with an assortment of enlarged photographs of King Kelly doing what he did best almost 50 years ago - - playing basketball.

King Kelly and Wayland still set off alarms even in borderline basketball fans across Kentucky and in neighboring states.

Bobby Hamilton says curiosity still gets the best of travelers on Hwy.80 who see the "Wayland" sign and the arrow pointing to Hwy. 7. He gets visitors on a regular basis to his service station located on King Kelly Coleman Highway asking about that 1956 team and King Kelly.

"They come by here all the time asking what ever happened to him," Hamilton says. "I tell 'em to stick around, that if he's in town he'll stop at the post office across the street and then come on over here. They really like to look at all of these pictures."

Those travelers who do make their way to Wayland will notice a collection of abandoned buildings and houses, covered in vines. Many of their roofs have collapsed with only the walls still standing. There's an assortment of cars, trucks, and a few appliances that sit just off the edge of the highway. From the looks of things they've been there for a long time.

Many of the residents that were there in the mid-50's have died, others have moved away to find employment. Still, those who have stayed around are quick to point out the good things Wayland has going for it, and do, indeed, see light at the end of the tunnel. And they say it's not the light from a train pulling the hundreds of train cars parked at the edge of town.

For many in this day and time the future is where it's at. There are those who ask why are we living in the past? Why are we talking about a team and especially a player who played fifty years ago?

The answer is quite simple.

It's about who we are. It's about overcoming odds to be successful. It's about doing something that will be remembered for generations to come, and it's about hope. It's a hope that says, "If they can do it, so can we."

The success of basketball in this Floyd County town in a certain way gave every person who lived there some hope. And if you don't have hope what do you have? One may wonder about Wayland's future, but one thing you don't have to wonder about is the town's past.

This small town, whose economy was fueled by the very coal it dug out of the ground, was a basketball town. It produced the greatest scoring machine never seen before or since. It's Wayland's claim to fame.

The King Kelly story has faded a bit over the years, but there's still this mystique. What is fact and what is fiction? The stories that have evolved have become legendary.

The echoes of the Wayland Wasps and King Kelly extend beyond a basketball team and its star player.

Chapter 2

The coal town of Wayland, Kentucky is located on Ky 7 and Ky 1086 some 25 miles south of Prestonsburg, the county seat of Floyd County. About one and a half miles from town is the Knott County boundary line. Knott County would play a key role in that legendary season for the Wayland Wasps in 1956.

Geographically, Wayland is an L-shaped town. Ky 7 runs parallel with the right fork of Beaver Creek, and Ky 1086 runs perpendicular to Ky 7 and parallel with Steele's Creek, tributary of Right Beaver Creek. The mouth of Steele's Creek forms the corner on the right angle of the L of Wayland.

The portion of the area that is now Wayland was settled in the early 1800s. Sometime around 1910 various land speculators began buying land and mineral rights throughout Eastern Kentucky. Gibson Coal and Coke was buying much of the land and soon after, they were taken over by Beaver Consolidated Coal which was absorbed by Elkhorn Coal Corporation.

The name Wayland was officially put in place for the coal camp in 1912 as a result of West Virginia U.S. Senator Clarence Wayland Watson who later became president of Elkhorn.

The only means for the transportation of goods, equipment and minerals was either by flat boats on the creek or in wagons on the underdeveloped roadways that looked more like trails. It was then that Elkhorn and Beaver Railroad, a subsidiary of the Chesapeake and Ohio began securing right-of-ways from area farmers and land owners. As land was purchased, laborers, made up primarily of Italian immigrants, laid tracks up Right Beaver that were eventually to end in Wayland with only a spur line leading to the nearby mines. Then, with the railroad's completion, and shipments of building materials and mining equipment fully underway, the construction of Wayland, the town, began.

Crudely fashioned streets were put in place, soon followed by a row of large frame duplexes, or double-houses as the locals called them. Each of these duplexes had two bedrooms upstairs, a kitchen and living room downstairs, and each was fitted with both a front and back porch equally divided by a banister down the middle. Outdoor latrines, referred to as toilets, privies or outhouses, were located behind each structure. At the middle of the back porch of the houses was a trough through which wastewater would be disposed. Also, on the edge of the back porches were little platform extensions for garbage cans to sit.

In 1939 Elkhorn replaced three smaller tipples with a huge, very modern one. These tipples were the heart of coal preparation and production once the coal was removed from the mines. The nation's demand for coal was growing and Wayland was keeping pace.

With the building of this new plant, the logo of Elkhorn Coal Corporation and the mascot of Wayland, the town, became the Wasp.

In order to support and help run the ever-growing mine operations, several shops sprang up. Among them was a carpenters shop. Company carpenters built porches, roofed houses, and made other repairs as reported by the town's renters. A blacksmith shop, supply shop and repair shop soon followed.

At the end of Front Street was a bathhouse with showers and lockers where the miners would bathe and change clothing at the end of their shift before going home. Up the hill a bit, just above the bath house, was the mine's laboratory, where an on site chemist analyzed the coal's content. And then a little further up the hill at what is called Shop Fork, a long hollow across Steele's Creek, was where the African American Elkhorn employees lived. Like the white workers, their houses were duplexes and, likewise, this community had a company store, a church and a school. These black families were allowed to attend movies at the Wayland Theater albeit they were required to sit on the back rows. Tickets were 20 cents for children and 40 cents for adults.

The movies were an outlet for the town's residents. It took their mind off of the hard, dangerous and low paying work most of the families experienced. In the 1920's it was the silents, before the talkies were introduced. The 40's and 50's were big for moviegoers in Wayland. Saturdays showcased Hopalong Cassidy, Tim Holt, the Durango Kid, Rocky Lane, and, of course, Roy Rogers and Gene Autry. On Sunday it was, for the most part, first run comedies, musicals and romances. During the mid-week they could watch B movies, often starring the likes of Ronald Reagan, Randolf Scott and George Montgomery.

In Wayland, Elkhorn built several single-family houses, reserved for company officials including the mining superintendent's house, as well as a church and parsonage.

Unlike many coal towns in Kentucky and West Virginia, Wayland residents cooked and heated their homes with natural gas, and the houses were equipped with electricity. In those early years, Elkhorn's generators provided electricity on a limited basis each day. Later it was available 24 hours a day.

Elkhorn's sanitation crews collected garbage on a regular schedule and even cleaned out the latrines. The company furthermore encouraged its renters to keep their porches and yards clean and neat, and most planted flowers in the front and vegetable gardens in the back.

In the 1940's baseball was big in Wayland, and although the town had a field, it was the new one that created some excitement in 1948, especially when then major league baseball commissioner A.B. "Happy" Chandler came to town to dedicate the new park. It was where Wayland's team played their Mountain League home games, and it was even lighted.

Those lights were bought with money acquired when union workers worked one Saturday and then contributed what they earned to the baseball project. Francis and Herman "Doc" Harmon then installed the lights. It was a wonderful community project and everyone was proud. Unfortunately there no longer is even the slightest hint that a baseball park once stood in a now vacated field just outside of the main part of town.

Believe it or not there was a tennis court in downtown Wayland. It must have looked somewhat out of place in the early 1940's. At some point in that decade the court was converted into a fence-enclosed outdoor basketball court. Surely in the years to come there would be more youngsters shooting baskets than working on their backhands. Who knows, some of those kids might be able to make the team over at the high school someday.

Much of Waylands social life revolved around the Fountain. In the old days it sat where Bobby Hamilton's Wayland Kwik Mart now sits. At the Fountain you could get a cheeseburger and a coke for less than 50 cents and almost always there as something playing on the nickel jukebox.

But life in Wayland was not a bed of roses by any stretch of the imagination. Always on their minds was the fear of a mine's roof collapse or some other mine disaster. The reality of danger was always with the miners and their families. A whistle from the mine at anytime other than the beginning of a new shift caused the townspeople to stand still as they frantically wondered what had happened. Was the injured or dead miner a husband, father, brother or a son?

It was a tough life. Not only was there the worry of accidents, but economic setbacks were also a reality. The "feast or famine" nature of the coal business always threatened a slowdown or even a complete shutdown. Occasionally a miner might get only two or three days work per week. And worse, they might even be laid off. Sometimes the United Mine Workers would call for a strike that would prove to be devastating to many of the miners and their families. During the strike many miners would use up their wages and had no savings. Those who had savings would usually exhaust them before the strike ended.

If that were not enough, always lurking in the back of Wayland residents was the possibility of flooding. If it rained for more than a few hours, they began to get nervous.

Because of its position at the mouth of Steel's Creek and on right Beaver Creek, Wayland is prone to flooding. Several times floods have wrought thousands of dollars in damage to property owners, and even though many of the town's buildings have been raised above the infamous 1937 flood level, the continuous filling over the years of Beaver Creek has caused heavy rains to rise higher and higher. With no method of flood control, it appears Wayland's future in dealing with rising water is not good.

In the early days roads were pretty much non-existent, and those that were there were generally impassible during the winter. The primary source of transportation was by train, and, because of this, the miners that came to work there brought their household goods and furniture in a boxcar. The families would arrive in passenger cars.

Thank goodness, roads did get better. Soon after one was completed up Right Beaver Creek, the Sparks Brother Bus Line began scheduled runs from Prestonsburg to Wayland to Hazard. Finally, Wayland was connected to the rest of the world. The new bus line made it possible for Wayland residents to visit friends, shop, or make connections with Greyhound busses that could transport them any where in the country.

Eventually the town had its own local transportation. George Hart drove the city's bus for a period of time. The fare was five cents and made round-trips from Wayland to Garrett, and from Wayland to Shop Fork and Stamper's Branch. Some of the youngsters would spend their nickels just to ride around town and up and down the hollows.

Elkhorn Coal Corporation provided the Wayland residents with a well-stocked company store. It might seem that everyone in Wayland did indeed work the mines, but it was not the case. The Kentucky-West Virginia Gas Company had several employee/residents, as did the railroad. There, of course, was a sprinkling of residents who owned or worked for other businesses in town.

But make no mistake, this was Elkhorn's town, and the company store was the heartbeat of Wayland. It was more like an early day Wal-Mart. Customers could purchase meat, poultry, dairy products, and fresh produce. Dry goods, including bolts of material, clothing, lingerie and linens were available. So was jewelry, shoes, boots, patent medicines, cosmetics, household furnishings and decorator items, appliances, groceries, tools, water buckets, laundry tubs, saddles, feed, seed, and even a coffin.

At the company store, purchase could be made with script (a company issued money), cash or lease. Furniture, school clothing and Christmas gifts could be bought on leases. A lease allowed employees to buy needed or desired merchandise on credit. The debt would be repaid through payroll deductions.

Elkhorn paid its workers in cash. Often a miner, after payroll deductions that included rent, utilities, leases and taxes, would open an empty yellow pay envelope.

What did it mean to be born in Wayland, or for that matter any coal camp owned by a coal company? In Wayland a child was brought into the world by a company doctor, in a company house, in a company town. His food was purchased at a company store, using company script by working long hours in the company mine. The school he attended was taught by a company teacher. The church he worshipped in was company owned, and when he died he went to the cemetery in a company wagon.

Chapter 3

Guy Coleman, Kelly's dad, came to Wayland from Pike County when he was 14 years old to do what every other man did then. . . work in the mines. The year was 1920, and he found a home in the back part of Bill Cooley's general store, just on the other side of Beaver Creek in the community of Glo.

Kelly's mom, Rusha, was from nearby Lackey. Her father Sherman Collins had been sheriff in Garrett. Guy and Rusha were married in 1930 and soon after started adding to their family. Kelly was six years old when his grandfather died but he always remembered the stories he heard and the things he saw. The times were often violent. It was common in the late 40's for men to be armed on weekends.

There were shootings and sometimes men died. Guns and alcohol didn't mix well. Wayland was a tough town. The work was tough and so were the men. But for many in town, it was a great time of their lives.

Guy Coleman worked hard in the mines and was well respected, and in June of 1953 he was elected Treasurer of the local United Mine Workers Union. He was a handsome man, standing close to 6' 2." Perhaps he could have been an outstanding athlete, but such an opportunity never came his way.

Kelly was the fifth born, following four sisters: Betty, Mary, Glenna and Phyllis. Next came Linda Carol, Priscilla, Phillip, Sandra, Keith and Peggy.

There were 11 children, and although they were never living in the same house at the same time, it took some creativity to raise such a large family in a two-bedroom house located on the right fork of Beaver Creek. The Coleman's took little comfort in knowing there were other families in Wayland living with the same circumstances.

The Coleman home on Beaver Creek was built on wooden posts, for there were times when the water would rise and they would be protected. There were also times, however, when the family had to move everything to the second floor until the water receded.

The 1952 green Studebaker truck that Guy owned served his family well. The smaller kids would pile in the back and two of the larger ones would sit in the front with their dad. Rusha Coleman didn't drive and, in fact, spent much of her time at home or at the Old Regular Baptist Church in Knott County just across the county line. It was common in the 1930's, 40's and even into the 50's for women not to drive. Back then driving was no big deal. Only a few families owned a car or truck. Roads were dirt or gravel, and besides, where was there to go. After all, they had everything they needed in life right there at the company store. If someone from Wayland said he was going to "town," it usually meant Prestonsburg.

At one time in the late 40's there was even a stop light in Wayland. Nobody was really sure why. Anyway, the Turner brothers eventually took care of that. They would shoot it out every Saturday night. Finally someone realized they didn't need a stop light after all.

Wayland was not without some of the other necessities that help make a town a town. The Bank of Wayland sat right in the middle of town on Hwy 7, and the Wayland Hotel was just down the street. It was the largest structure in town with 12 rooms. It also had a restaurant, beauty shop, barber shop and poolroom. But in 1953 the town was in its "feast" phase and often outsiders came to Wayland to do business with Elkhorn that on occasion would require an overnight. The Fraley-Dearing Chevrolet dealership took care of the residents new and used car needs. Of course the Fountain was where one socialized, mainly the younger folks. A hamburger and Pepsi cost 25 cents.

Back then there were the two poolrooms. Charlie Gray owned one of them and he had strict instructions from Guy Coleman that "if you see my son Kelly in here, chase him out."

Life for many Wayland residents was about to change. For all practical purposes it had been good for the some 3,600 citizens. In some ways it was a mirror of what was socially happening throughout the rest of Kentucky. Work or you and your family didn't eat.

But what happened when the work opportunities went away?

In the mid to late1940's Elkhorn Coal began to offer the renters of their company houses an opportunity to own their own homes. It sounded good. Who wouldn't want to be a homeowner? Work was pretty good. For the time being the miners were getting a full work load, and some were even getting extra time.

Later miners and families would say, "We should have known. It seemed to good to be true."

For all practical purposes coal mining in Wayland had ended by 1954. The tipple was leased to another company, and years later torn down. Over the next several years, the original Fountain, the Wayland Hotel, the hospital, company store and the theater would also be gone.

People were moving away in droves, and for good reason, to find work. Most miners left their families behind. After all, they owned a house in Wayland. They were out of work and had house payments to make.

Guy Coleman was among those leaving to find work. When the mines had been cleaned out there was a migration northward to Ohio, Indiana, Illinois and Michigan where many began new lives with new careers.

Guy settled in Cleveland. The work was steady and the pay was decent. When he was sure things would work out he would sell his house in Wayland and the family would join him. He would do his best to get back home every two or three months.

Kelly was a sophomore at Wayland High and for the most part was now on his own. His mother had her hands full with his six younger brothers and sisters at home, and Kelly was free to pretty much do as he pleased, including shooting pool down at Charlie Gray's Pool Room.

Kelly was a free-spirit before the term became popular years later. Some might say he was out of control. He ran with whomever he wanted to, and drank beer much like many his age did in Wayland in 1954.

It fell on Copper John Campbell, his coach, to provide any influence in his life if there was going to be any at all.

Chapter 4

Even though the Wayland Wasps were coming off of only a five-win season in 1953, Copper John Campbell knew he had something special going. He had a star in the making.

The Wayland coach had, himself, been successful as a player. At Hindman, he was all-state, leading his team to the championship game in 1939, losing to Brooksville 43-39. He was the game's high scorer with 13.

Campbell went on to Eastern Kentucky University in Richmond and was a standout for the Colonels.

Wayland, as a school, had tasted basketball success before Coleman arrived. In 1947, Edd DeCoursey, an all-stater, led Wayland to the Sweet Sixteen where they lost in the first round 56-53 to an Owensboro team whose roster had a young player on the verge of becoming a star - - Cliff Hagan.

Wayland and all-state Fred Fraley returned in 1951, advancing to the quarterfinals by trouncing Lyon County 82-47. Louisville Manual sent the Wasps back home with a 77-45 defeat.

So at 33 years of age Copper John Campbell, the coach, knew what success was all about and what it would take to get back to Sweet Sixteen.

He knew with Kelly Coleman heading into his sophomore year and emerging as a legitimate star, things were looking up.

In 1954, Coleman upped his scoring average to 26 points, and Wayland finished the year 19-7. But, mountain basketball was loaded with great teams.

Hindman, Pikeville, Inez and Hazard were just a few of the powers. Night in and night out these teams could play with the best. Quickly, Wayland was joining that group, mainly because of one player.

Inez, behind the play of Billy Ray Cassady and Herbie Triplett, swept through the state tournament beating Newport 63-55 for the 1954 championship.

Many observers felt like 1955 was going to be Wayland's year. They had four returning senior starters, plus Kelly. Big things were expected.

By now the entire state was beginning to hear and read about the scoring machine from Wayland. He was scoring points at an unheard of pace. He was pretty much unstoppable.

"My junior year was the first time I started shooting a jump shot," Kelly said. "I practiced it a long time before I used it in a game."

The *Courier-Journal* and *Louisville Times* were starting to report Coleman's feats to other parts of the state. Down in Lexington, the *Herald-Leader* was regularly reporting on what kind of night Coleman had.

But it was writer/stringer Gordon Moore from Prestonsburg who first told the rest of the world about the 6' 3," 215 pound manchild from Wayland. "Bar none he was the best to ever play in the mountains," said Moore, who covered eastern Kentucky basketball for 30 years for the Courier-Journal. Moore saw Coleman first as a freshman and was very much aware that he never really took advantage of his "God-given talent." "He just never really had to work at it to be good," added Moore. "As good as he was there's no telling how good he could have been or what he could have accomplished if he would have had a little leadership and encouragement from home."

For Kelly's parents, watching him play basketball was not a priority.

There were other things more important. Like taking care of the other kids, and working to put food on the table. It was a hard life for many who lived in the coal towns, and although some found the games over at the Wayland gym a way to forget about these troubles, such was not the case for Guy and Rusha.

Rusha would hear all of the talk about Kelly, and she was proud. But she was proud of all her children.

By Kelly's junior year his confidence was just as big as his game. For the year he racked up 1,174 points while averaging 33 points. It was a new state scoring record, but Wayland's season came to an end in the regional semi's when they lost to a Donnis Butcher-led Meade Memorial team.

A 29-7 record, although good, left a bittersweet taste.

Coleman said they expected to do better. "We were disappointed. Our best defensive player, Hubert Hall, got too old and was not allowed to play in the tournament," he said in referring to the "19-year old rule."

But once again a mountain team prevailed, winning it all in Lexington.

Hazard, led by Johnny Cox, a future UK All-American, made it two in a row for mountain schools.

Chapter 5

n Kelly's earlier years, it was pretty much expected that he would do what many mountain players had done before him – go downstate to Lexington and play for Adolph Rupp at the University of Kentucky.

Wah-Wah Jones from Harlan, Billy Ray Cassady from Inez and Johnny Cox from Hazard had all come from the mountains and done well for the Wildcats.

But there was another team from the mountains that wanted Kelly to play for them. The Mountaineers from the University of West Virginia in Morgantown had had their eye on Wayland for sometime. A young coach named Fred Schaus was in the process of assembling a group of players to make a run at a national championship.

The Elkhorn Coal Company in Wayland was headquartered out of Charleston, West Virginia and it hadn't taken long for word to reach Schaus that he just might have the inside track on the best high school player in the nation - - Kelly Coleman.

Coleman had just finished a fantastic junior season in 1955 averaging almost 33 points a game, setting a new state scoring record. All of the starters, except him, graduated. Next year he thought, could be tough. So when West Virginia came calling and asked him to play his senior season at Greenbrier Military School in Lewisburg,

West Virginia, Kelly said he would think about it.

He thought about the team next year at Wayland. He thought about his coach, Copper John, and how he had worked with him even to the point of putting up with occasional behavior that others might not. He thought about his family and friends. He thought about his pretty girlfriend, Ann Watkins.

Kelly also knew he needed some discipline in his life, and maybe, just maybe, a military environment would be just what he needed. Greenbrier, a school that cost $2,000 a year, is where he headed.

The high school and townspeople of Wayland were crushed. After all, he had put them on the map. Anybody who was anybody had heard of Wayland and King Kelly, even if they didn't know exactly where it was.

Kelly's arrival at Greenbrier didn't go unnoticed by the other cadets. Not only did he look out of place in his uniform, he also felt out of place. Polished brass, straight gig lines, and spit-shined shoes were not his style.

"I got in a few fights," he said. "I didn't like taking orders. Hell, I was only 16 years old and it was something I wasn't used to."

School policy said 250 demerits and you were out. At Wayland, Kelly could dress the way he wanted, even go to school pretty much when he was ready, and on occasion a scuffle meant no more than a "break it up" from the coach. "I got my 250 demerits pretty quick," he recalls. "The Commandant called me and the coach in and told me they would wipe the slate clean if I'd straighten up and behave."

There was no way he was going to stay. Thanks but no thanks and he was on his way back to Wayland. He had lasted six weeks.

A 14-hour train ride delivered a worn out Kelly

Coleman to Allen, Kentucky where his family picked him and his one suitcase up and drove him back to Wayland.

The King was back.

Chapter 6

Kelly Coleman had become bigger than life, but he was able to back it up. King Kelly was like a great big action hero, and the mountains loved it. He was a sportswriters dream. They kept writing, and as his on-court heroics and off-court antics spread, he was fast approaching cult status.

As much hoopla as Kelly was getting about his scoring he was also getting quite a bit of attention about his love for food, drink and girls.

His pre-game meal was a couple of burgers, and a shake, usually at the Fountain. When asked if such a diet just before a game bothered him, he answered, "Apparently not."

Some said Kelly was drinking a lot more than just shakes.

One of the good stories was the night Wayland was playing Maytown. During a timeout one of the Maytown players complained to his coach, Ed Stewart, that Kelly was under the influence. He could smell alcohol and he was sure the Wayland star was drunk. Coach Stewart told the player to "find out what brand Kelly was drinking, because he's already scored 52 on us."

King Kelly finished the game with 75 points and 41 rebounds.

"That stuff was exaggerated," Coleman said. "I never drank during a game. Our team was accused of having more than just water in our bottles, but it wasn't so. Now don't get me wrong, after the game was a different story."

But wait a minute. There may have been some truth about that Maytown defender smelling liquor on Kelly's breath. Frankie Francis was a sophomore player at nearby Garrett High School that year. It just so happened that his team didn't have a game that night, so he and a buddy were hitchhiking to Wayland to see the King play.

"We were at Mullins Service Station in Estill about a mile and a half from Wayland, looking for a ride," laughed Francis. "Apparently you could get a lot more than gas at Mullin's," as Frances continued. "Kelly walked in and said he wanted a half pint. I think he gave Mr. Mullins a couple of bucks. It was a bottle of Bond-Lillard. Kelly twisted the cap off, took a big swig, put the cap on and threw it in the waste can. As he was walking out the door Mr. Mullins said, 'Hey King, how many you gonna get tonight?' Kelly looked back over his shoulder and said, 'sixty-five.'"

Francis, who later coached Wheelwright High School from 1966 to 1976, recalled those "three-on-three cut-throat pick up games" on the outdoor court at Wayland. "I was younger and I was just glad they let me play. We played for Pepsi's and the game was to 16," recalled Francis. "If you got on Kelly's team you drank a lot of Pepsi's."

Francis remembered how hard Kelly played, even in pick-up games.

"He was such a competitor," he said. "He worked on his change of pace jump shot. And, I do remember, when Kelly decided to leave, so did the crowd."

There was also a story about Kelly, early in his sophomore year, catching a ride to the gym. The driver offered him some tequila. Four or five drinks later when he got to the gym he was lucky to get his uniform on.

"I made two goals that night," said Coleman.

Gordon Moore, the writer, knew Coleman well. Although several people have taken credit, it was Moore who hung the "King" label on Kelly Coleman.

"I resented it. I was just a kid," says Coleman. "Think about it. Why would anybody want that?"

Kelly was no dummy though. He knew what the fans wanted and he knew he could do it - - score.

But what was basketball giving to Kelly in the mid-50's, when his dad was bringing home $50.00 per month working in the coal mines? King Kelly's success meant dignity, respect, acceptance, and attention for him and his family. It came with a price however, because it was the attention Coleman had trouble living with away from the court.

Moore says Kelly drank too much back then, and that he lacked that one person to push him in the right direction. Even in spite of that he still played basketball better than anyone else.

Most of Kentucky is made up of small towns. From one end of the state to the other it's tobacco, bourbon, horses or coal, but its one common thread is basketball. Basketball fans everywhere couldn't get enough of King Kelly.

Copper John Campbell was satisfied that, even with Kelly being the only returning starter, Wayland could be very good.

Don't forget, Coleman started the year at Greenbrier Military School in West Virginia. It could have been a disastrous season. Coach Campbell got another break when Billy Ray Fultz transferred in from Wheelwright. Although Fultz has never played on an organized team he looked good in practice and would be a starter.

Billy Ray Combs had never played on a team before either, but senior Elmond Hall and sophomore Melvin Robinson had, and they were pretty good. They knew their roles - - get the ball to Kelly and get out of the way. But, and it was a big but, be ready just in case. Before the season was over they would have their chance.

Everybody wanted to see Kelly play. Many who couldn't, wrote letters, lots of them. Some even sent him money because they had read he was from the mountains. The perception was, if you're from the mountains you must be poor, and if you're poor you must need money. That was OK with Kelly.

With all that was good in Wayland, there was also some bad.

Any college that was anything in basketball wanted the King. Out of state license plates in and around Floyd County were common to see. They weren't there to look at the mountains.

Kelly scored so many points at such a pace that gamblers gave odds on how many points he would get against a particular team.

He scored over 50 points on twelve occasions his senior year, including that 75-point game against Maytown. It became big news when he didn't score 50.

Pearl Combs, the coach over at Hindman was so certain that Kelly wasn't going to have a big night against his team that he boasted that the Wayland player might get 25. The reported betting line was 35 points.

When the yellow school bus pulled up in front of the Hindman gym, Coach Combs greeted Copper John and the Wayland team. As Kelly walked by him, the coach informed him that tonight they were going to "hold him to 25." "Which quarter?" Kelly replied as he kept walking.

Kelly had 39 at the half.

"When I walked out of the gym that night, some of those guys congratulated me and when they shook my hand, there'd be a bill in mine," Kelly said.

The King was 17-years-old and West Virginia still wanted him to play basketball in Morgantown.

Most of King Kelly's shots were taken from the top of the key. He was pure, a fantastic shooter, and although his shot was not picture perfect, the end result usually was. He didn't need but a split second to get free from the defender and fire his shot from slightly toward his right shoulder.

Copper John was asked why he let Kelly shoot so much. "Well, the name of the game is basketball, and no one puts it in the basket better than Kelly," he responded.

For his size and apparent bulk his speed was deceptive. He dribbled with an effortless style, and with a stop and go move he left the defender, like everyone else in the gym, watching the ball go through the net.

One writer described Kelly's moves as that of a Sherman tank. Another said he would bull his way to the basket after running over several defenders.

Coleman says that wasn't the case at all. "They did everything to stop me, they grabbed my uniform, stepped on my toes, pushed and shoved," he said. "It didn't matter. It still didn't work. I could stop on a dime and most of the time they'd fall down and I'd have an open shot."

Those games were not for the faint of heart. The fans were vocal, sometimes with language that for sure wouldn't be heard on Sunday at Rusha's Baptist Church. The conversation on the floor among the players was often R-rated, too. Back then they didn't call it trash talk.

"It was all about holding your own, holding your ground," says Kelly almost 50 years later. "It's difficult to remember everything that was said, but I do know that I couldn't let the opposition know they were getting to me."

But for all of the things said and written about the King, the one common denominator, the one common thing they say about him was his ability to follow his shot. When he did miss from outside, he had an uncanny knack for getting the rebound and putting it in the basket.

"I can't explain it, he offered." "I don't know how I did it."

Chapter 7

Even though he had given up military life at Greenbrier Academy, West Virginia hadn't given up on him.

"I had a sponsor who made sure I had what I needed," Kelly said. "A car, money and clothes, and several high schools tried to say I was ineligible when I came back to Wayland."

For most of Kentucky, their high school team was the town's heart and soul. Consolidations had not yet ripped the fabric from each of the small communities. There were more than 600 high schools then (275 today) and when the home team played, everyone knew what everyone else would be doing that night. . . going to the game. And in Wayland, even when Beaver Creek escaped its banks because of March rains, they'd even go by boat.

The game was it. And even though Kelly was the only returning starter from the previous year, big things were expected. They would not disappoint.

Arguably, before consolidation, eastern Kentucky produced more great teams than any part of the state.

Sportswriter Dave Kindred quoted one basketball fan saying," In eastern Kentucky, if a lump of coal ain't Jesus Christ, basketball is."

Mountain basketball was, if not a religion, most certainly a way of life. Very little was more important. The community and its basketball team was the single factor that brought the people together.

Coach Copper John Campbell breathed a sigh of relief upon his star player's return. Even though it was not a perfect relationship, they respected each other. There was a lot of give and take. As good as he was, Kelly's antics sometimes created a little rub on his teammates, too. But, not the fans. They loved it all.

In Kindred's book, *Basketball, The Dream Game In Kentucky*, Copper John offered that newspapers used too much ink on Coleman. "It made him feel his Cheerios, if you know what I mean."

There was a time when principal Lawrence Price went to the coach and suggested that he might want to consider sitting Kelly down for a game in order to "reel him in a bit." Copper John said he valued Mr. Price's life too much to do that. "What do you mean," Price asked the coach. Copper John told him if word got out that Price had kept Kelly from playing "your life wouldn't be worth a plugged nickel." Price replied, "In that case we'd better play him."

Kelly's first experience with basketball ended in a major disappointment. As an eighth grader he was cut from the B-team. That next summer Kelly shared his love of baseball with lots of time working on his basketball game.

It paid off.

He made the B-team his freshman year, but Coach Campbell quickly moved him to the varsity where he rode the bench for the first two games of the season.

"I didn't play at all," said Coleman. "I was very frustrated."

All of that was about to change, however. In a script made for the movies, Copper John, for some reason, decided to start Kelly in the third game of the year.

In pure Hollywood style, he scored 27 points in the very

first game he ever played. It was Wayland's first win of the season. They would win only five games that year, but Kelly went on to earn All-District honors, and by his own admission didn't even know what All-District meant.

For the year he averaged 19 points a game.

He was only 14-years-old.

Bob Daniels was a senior All-State player at Oil Springs High School in nearby Johnson County the year Kelly was a freshman.

"I remember our coach telling us they had a good young player who could score," says Daniels. "At the time I didn't remember his name. It was later, of course, I realized who he was." Daniels went on to have an outstanding basketball and baseball career at Western Kentucky University and years later their paths would cross again.

Chapter 8

The team itself would be an oddity. There really wasn't a team chemistry. The boys didn't know each other all that well.

Because mountain roads were so bad in the 50's, five of the boys rode a school bus in from neighboring Knott County. It was easier, quicker and safer to bus to Wayland in Floyd County than to one of the Knott County schools where they lived. So, after the Knott County boys got their practice in, they would be on a bus headed home, not sticking around to socialize.

Starters Billy Ray Combs, Melvin Robinson and Elmond Hall were from Knott as were subs Jackie Thornberry and James Vernon Hall. Kelly was the only starter actually from Wayland. Freshman Curtis Ray Slone, Afton Bates, Bobby Bentley, and Jackie Greathouse also lived in Wayland. Billy Ray Fultz had just moved from Wheelwright.

Hubert Hall and Lowell Gibson had given Kelly a lot of support the year before, but even with them they couldn't overcome a Donnis Butcher Meade Memorial team and had been knocked out of the regional tournament.

There was no question about it, if Wayland was to meet the expectations of everyone who had heard about them and their great scoring star, Kelly Coleman, Copper John had some work to do.

Kelly had broken the state scoring record as a junior by averaging over 32 points a game, and as Copper John liked to say about him, "he likes to feel his Cheerios, if you know what I mean."

Kelly on one hand was shy, but on the other he was very confident. He was a marked man, he knew it, and relished it.

Whenever Wayland played, college coaches flocked. Wayland had had good players before. Edd DeCoursey and Fred Fraley had packed them in several years before, but it was not like this.

One thing is for sure, Copper John Campbell, as a coach, never has received the credit for keeping it all together. It would take a certain kind of coach, with a certain kind of personality and disposition to deal with the day-to-day pressures of coaching Kelly and convincing his Wasp teammates of their roles on the team if they were to achieve success. Expectations were high.

Wayland opened the season as expected, winning four in a row including a 70-68 win over powerhouse neighbor Carr Creek.

• • •

What was it like to have played with Kelly, to be his teammate in high school, to practice with him? What did his teammates remember?

Melvin Robinson was the starting center on that 1956 team, and though only a sophomore, he averaged 16 points a game.

"We were just average ballplayers, plus Kelly," Robinson says. "No one was jealous of him. We all just played. Kelly got the credit, but he knows we helped a lot."

Robinson remembered his team never worked much on defense in practice or ran many set offensive plays.

James Vernon Hall was a center on the team, and though not a starter, the 6'3" senior remembered years later that Kelly seemed to practice when he wanted. "He'd shoot a few and leave," Hall said, "but of course he didn't need as much practice as the rest of us."

Hall had his own take about all the points Kelly scored. "Heck, we averaged over 91 points a game. Kelly would get half of them and the rest of us would get the other half. No one resented him."

Jackie Thornberry was also a senior on that team and according to him, as a sub he had the best seat in the house from which to watch Kelly play. "Our senior year Kelly was such a celebrity," he says. "I don't know how he handled it as well as he did. They should have left him alone."

Thornberry continued, "We knew we were pretty good when the principal gave lunch tickets to the whole team. That free lunch, plus the 50 cents a day I got from my parents, was a good deal."

Billy Ray Fultz had moved to Wayland from Wheelwright, and although he had never played on an organized team, he had impressed Copper John enough to be a starter. His specialty was defense and rebounding.

"We just had fun playing," said Fultz. "Kelly was simply the best and with him we knew we had a chance to beat any team."

Curtis Ray Slone was a freshman on that team and had dressed for the varsity as an eighth grader.

After high school, Slone, over the years, has lived in Wheelwright, Morehead and Newport, and the Wayland native says his claim to fame was that he played with Kelly Coleman. "Once they found out I was from Wayland, people would ask me what was it like playing with Kelly. I just told them he was the greatest."

Slone today is a barber in Wayland and regularly cuts Kelly's hair.

There was another freshman that was a part of the team that year in 1956. Shirell Hall was, along with senior Jackie Collins, the team manager. Managers sometime have a different perspective on things. They see and hear things that others on the team don't. Their main job at practice was to make sure the basketballs and a few towels were on the court when practice started.

"We carried the balls in an old army duffle bag," recalled Hall. "It was our job to make sure the balls were kept clean, and sometime we would polish 'em. I do remember that most of our guys liked for the basketballs to be a little rough, not too slick. We were used to playing outside and that's the way the balls were."

Hall's dad, Fred, was the president of the local Elkhorn Coal in Wayland, so Copper John was using good politics when he asked the younger Hall to be one of the managers. After all, when school was out for the summer, it was Elkhorn who employed the coach. Copper John knew what he was doing.

Hall also kept the scorebook on all the road games that year.

"As I look back on it," he said, "I had a great seat to see one of the all-time greats. I do remember at practice there would be times when Coach and Kelly would get into it with each other. It was just a part of it. Coach would talk to him about his defense. 'At least put your hands up', he would yell at Kelly."

Chapter 9

As much publicity as Coleman received, there were others across the state that played the games pretty well, too.

Following Coleman's breakout junior year at Wayland, coaches throughout Kentucky wanted to schedule marque games, games that would feature the best teams and best players against each other.

In 1956 when the schedules were released the teams hadn't been announced for the annual Central City Invitational. This Muhlenburg County coal town in western Kentucky not only had the Peabody Coal Company, the Everly Brothers, but also one of the best basketball players in the nation.

Raymond Withrow went by the name of Corky and he was good, very good. Fans in the western part of the state had to look no further than Brewers in 1948, Owensboro in 1945 and Cuba in 1952 for past state champions, so they didn't give any ground when it came to turning out great high school basketball.

So when Central City announced that Wayland and Kelly Coleman would be coming to town the entire state took notice. East versus West. Coal town against coal town. Kelly against Corky. Forget that there would be eight other players on the court. It didn't seem to matter. But in the end it did.

A packed house at Central City High School was not unusual back then. Central City was good, and basketball in Muhlenburg County was about as good as it would ever be.

Five miles down the road from Central City was Greenville High School. Many who followed the game back then said their star, Roger Newman, was the best of all. Withrow and Newman played in the same district, so there was always a chance one of their teams wouldn't even make it to the regionals, depending on the draw.

But this tournament on December 23 and 24 in 1955 was only about Coleman and Withrow. Forget everything else.

Coleman remembers his coach, Copper John Campbell, one day at practice telling him he had gotten a call from Central City inviting Wayland to play in their tournament. "I remember the season had already started when coach asked me what I thought about playing there," Coleman recalled. "We knew they were good, but we also knew it would be tough to win. The deck would be stacked. The officiating would probably be bad, and, besides that it was all the way across the state." Wayland went anyway.

In the opening round Central City defeated Todd County 85-63 and Wayland, behind Coleman's 40 points, turned back Graham 65 to 53.

One of the big things to do in Central City was shoot pool, and with four pool halls on the main drag of town, a person had his choice. It just so happened that it was the Central Pool Room where just by chance the Wayland Wasps and Central City Golden Tide ended up together on the morning before the championship game.

Corky Withrow remembers somewhat of a turf invasion.

"The Central was where we always went to shoot pool," says Withrow. "We walked in and there was Kelly and his team." "We didn't say anything and they didn't either. They stared at us and we stared at them. That's the way it was back then, good or bad. They were the enemy."

That night was something to see. Fans began lining up outside the gym to buy tickets at 2:00 p.m. for a game that tipped off at 7 p.m. It was Christmas Eve and those that were there were looking for an early gift. Two of the state's better officials were working the game, Doc Ferrell and Don "Quack" Butler.

Robbie Harper told the *Times-Argus* newspaper in Central City several years later: "It was a big-time game. They came from everywhere to watch it. I remember standing in a long line a long time to get in."

Harper went on to describe Coleman as a great outside shooter. "He would shoot from around 24 feet and if he missed he had the uncanny ability to know which side of the rim the ball would go off on. He would then go get his own rebound and put it in the hole."

Jerry Young remembered years later the excitement of a full house and the anticipated duel between Coleman and Withrow. "He was a good size man, but he could still move," Young said of Coleman.

Clyde Stovall told the *Times-Argus* years later that he got to the game early and was surprised to see Coleman eating popcorn and drinking a Coke before the game. He said he had been told never to eat or drink before a game. Stovall also recalled that every time Coleman scored the crowd would scream for Withrow to match him. And he did, as each scored 40 that night.

Central City raced to 22-15 first quarter lead. The home team built a nine point second quarter lead, and early in the third upped it to 10. But Wayland and Kelly made a run, cutting the margin to four points. That's as close as they would get before losing 83-75. Withrow had had a great game defending as well, holding Melvin Robinson scoreless.

Before the Central City tournament began Copper John had described Kelly to Earl Cox of the *Courier-Journal* like this:

"His best shot is a driving jump shot from the back of the circle. He can drive through for lay-ups and is an excellent rebounder. Our opponents usually have two or three men guarding him. He is a master at shooting off balance. In 10 years of coaching, I have never seen a better high school player."

Like Coleman's, Withrow's life was not without its ups and downs, and also a little controversy after his high school years. In 1957 he signed a professional baseball contract with the Milwaukee Braves. This was after he had accepted a scholarship to play for UK. Back then if you signed a pro contract, regardless of what sport it was in, you were ineligible to play at a Division I NCAA school.

Goodbye, Kentucky.

Withrow then signed to play for Bullet Wilson at Kentucky Wesleyn, but soon was declared ineligible there, too, even though they were a Division II school. He finally landed at Georgetown College in Kentucky, an NAIA school.

"I thought I could at least play basketball now," said Withrow. "Back then Georgetown played Louisville every year and their coach, Peck Hickman said he wouldn't play us if I was allowed to play. This was all because I signed to play pro baseball. My sophomore year in 1959 I got to play against U of L and we beat them. That was the same year U of L beat Kentucky."

Withrow went on to have a somewhat undistinguished 10-year baseball career, mostly in the minors. He did make it to the majors when the St. Louis Cardinals brought him up in 1963.

"I guess the biggest highlight I had was my first at bat. It was against the Dodgers and pitcher Sandy Koufax, and then I was the guy that replaced Stan Musial in left field in the very last game he played. That game was at Wrigley Field in Chicago and their fans weren't very happy with me. They let me know it . . . threw half-eaten hot dogs, anything they could, at me. They had come to see Musial, not me."

Indeed, there were several similarities between Coleman and Withrow. Some thought it could have just as easily been King Corky, but the king was already taken.

Both were high school All-Americans in 1956, along with Oscar Robertson from Indianapolis, Indiana, and Jerry West from Cabin Creek, West Virginia.

The two were again on opposing sides when they took part in a series of East-West all-star games in eastern Kentucky.

The games were played in Pikeville, Paintsville and Whitesburg and Withrow was quick to point out that he and not Coleman was named Star of Stars after the games conclusion.

The pair did, however, become teammates for two games, the two-game series for the annual Kentucky-Indiana All-Star Game.

While Coleman came into the game recovering from a sprained ankle, overweight and out of shape, Withrow was suffering from food poisoning. With Kentucky's best not at full speed, Oscar Robertson put on a show, scoring 34 and 41 while leading Indiana to a two-game sweep.

In the first game Kelly led Kentucky with 17 while Corky added 13. Neither really showed up for the second game in Louisville. Kelly was 1-9 from the field and 2-2 free throws for four points. Corky didn't fare much better, 3-13 on field goals and 0-2 at the line for a total of six.

Louisville Central's Edgar Smallwood led Kentucky with 29.

"Rupp used those games against me when he was trying to get me to come to UK," Coleman said. "He said he didn't know really how good I was. I knew I could play. I knew I could play with anybody when I was healthy."

Chapter 10

As the season progressed, the loss to Central City did little to discourage Wayland and Kelly about their prospects for a state championship.

"I told Copper John then that we were setting ourselves up for a loss," Kelly says years later of the Central City game. "It was one of those made for publicity games that wasn't even on our schedule when the season started. We got publicity, but we also got a loss."

With that loss behind them the Wasps were ready to get back to the mountains and take care of business.

If you were seeing Wayland playing for the first time, not knowing anything about the team, not knowing who their best player was, you would probably not pick out Kelly Coleman during warm-ups. But once the game started, you knew almost instantly which one was the King.

It didn't matter that the socks drooped down over the top of his black Chuck Taylor's, or that his number 66 sweat-stained jersey was slightly pulled out, hanging over the waistband of his trunks. At 6' 3" and 215-pounds, the ruddy-complexioned youngster looked like he could be anything but a basketball player. But, he was. He knew it, and so did everyone else, which made Wayland's 800 seat gym a hot ticket.

"Many nights during one of our home games I'd look over and see people from Garrett, Maytown and Martin," says

Kelly. "Even when their team was playing on the same night, they all wanted to see us play."

Those who couldn't get a seat had to settle for the next best thing - - sitting outside in their cars in the school's parking lot. There was a small peep-hole at one end of the floor. Periodically someone standing in the "lobby" would check the score and report it to those sitting in their cars.

In some variation that's the way it probably was in hundreds of small towns across Kentucky on Tuesday and Friday nights. Towns lived and died on the outcome of basketball games played by teenagers. The games offered a chance for miners to forget about their tough, dirty and dangerous jobs in the mines. It was a chance for one town to earn bragging rights over another. These towns lived for those games. Every play, if not life and death, sure did seem like it.

In Wayland home crowds were rough. Grown men who had worked in the mines 10 hours a day, used the games to release tension and frustrations. Their language, often salty, was often directed at opposing teams, and, of course, referees. It was a common occurrence for fans who didn't see eye-to-eye inside the gym to continue their differences in the parking lot.

Before school consolidation, the small schools had evolved into something bigger than life. Player's were heroes and coaches were often viewed as God-like. Consolidation took that away.

The night of January 17, 1956, when Kelly got those 75 points and 41 rebounds against Maytown, must have been something to see. He almost outscored the entire Maytown team as Wayland won 105-79. Alcohol or not, he scored 31 field goals and hit 13-16 free throws. His points came on 21 in the first quarter, only eight in the second, and 23 each in the third and fourth. Thirty-two minutes of play with the clock stopping only for free throws, and no three-point goal, makes you wonder how many he would have scored by today's rules.

A few days later on January 24, Kelly came back with a 61-point game against Flat Gap. Wayland won 106-82. His points came on 20 field goals and 21 foul shots. It's not like Flat Gap was a nobody. Charlie Osborne, who later stared at Western Kentucky, scored 43 and future UK star Carroll Burchett had nine. Together, they were no match for Kelly.

The King was hot. He was the talk of the state.

Against Prestonsburg on January 31, Kelly outdualed all-stater Lowell Hughes as the Wasps won 107-80. Kelly had 63 points by way of 27 field goals and nine free throws. Hughes hit for 46 points on 18 field goals and 10 free throws.

Hughes, who went on to play baseball, football and basketball at Kentucky, remembers the official that night talking to him and Kelly before the game as the two captains met at mid court. "He said, 'boys there's lots of scouts here to see you play, so just go out there and give them what they came to see. Nobody's gonna foul out'," Hughes laughed. "I was determined to stop him but I couldn't. "He was so deceptive with his foot work. He'd get me backing up and it was all over."

On February 17, Kelly continued to add to the legend. It was for a game he almost didn't play.

"I told Copper John that I needed a game off," Kelly said. "The pressure of the season was really starting to wear on me and I needed to get away. If I didn't get 50 everyone wanted to know what was wrong."

The game Kelly would miss would be a road game at Wheelwright, a team the Wasps had lost to at home by 10 back in late November. However, the Wayland coach reasoned that his team was playing much better and their chances at Wheelwright, even without his star, were good. He gave Kelly permission to take the night off.

Kelly, however, had another reason for wanting to skip the game.

"I needed to go to Charleston, West Virginia and pick up a car that my sponsor, Mr. Hubert Kidd, had for me," Kelly said. "I was hitchhiking. It was really cold that night, and I was up near Louisa when this car came by headed back toward Wayland. Noah Howard, a big wheel with Elkhorn Coal, was driving. He had been to Huntington and turned around and picked me up and took me back to Wayland. It was cold and I was cold, so he didn't have to do much talking to get me in the car. He drove me to my house where I picked up my uniform and then on to Wheelwright."

He arrived at the halftime and his team was down by nine. "When I started the second half we got a technical foul," says Kelly. "I guess because I wasn't in the scorebook. They hit the foul shot and got the ball, too. We came back and won."

Wayland won 96-87 with Kelly scoring 33.

Wayland finished the regular season with a 26-5 record. The district tournament was next.

It was Copper John's policy before district and regional tournament games to put his team up in the Wayland hotel, where he could keep an eye on everyone, although it was common knowledge who he was really trying to watch. The coach probably thought his star might be "feeling his Cheerios."

It was somewhat ironic then when Copper John went by Rusha Coleman's house to tell her where her son would be staying so he could "watch out for them," she asked the coach how Kelly was doing and how many points he was scoring. Copper John assured her that Kelly was doing great, averaging 47 points a game. Rusha then asked, "Why do you want to change things now?"

In her wisdom it was her way of letting the coach know that she knew. You stick with what got you there. Why change the routine now?

The district was played at McDowell High School. Wayland cruised, taking care of Wheelwright 79-45 in the opener. Kelly scored 40. Martin was the next to fall, 100-68. Kelly's 57 points served notice he was gearing up. Wayland and Betsy Lane advanced to the finals. Both would move on to the regionals the next week in Pikeville, but Copper John wanted to make sure there were no slip-ups. He wanted to advance as a champion and not a runner-up. He didn't have to worry, as Wayland won 84-74. The King had 41 points.

Pikeville was the site of the 15th Regionals, and although Wayland would be the favorite to advance to the Sweet 16, most everyone knew the hometeam would be tough to beat. Besides that, they were pretty good. Led by H.L. Justice and Howard Lockhart, the John Bill Trivette coached team finished regular season and district play with a 21-7record.

But first things first. Wayland had an opening round game with a strong Betsy Lane team, whose best player was Thomas Spears.They were coached by Tommy Boyd and he knew all about Wayland. He had played for the Wasps. His team had defeated Copper John's at Wayland back in November, 90-80, and had lost to them 80-66 in the regular season, and then again in the district finals, 84-74. He also knew that the Wasps were not just a one-man team in spite of Kelly's stats. There was not another player like the King for sure, but Boyd knew Wayland had some other players on the team he had to pay attention to. Do you let Kelly get his and concentrate on the others? Or do you put two or three on Kelly and hope, just hope, the other four don't beat you?

Elmond Hall came into the tournament averaging 16 points a game. On many teams he would have been the star, the go-to-guy. Hall was underrated and had a knack of rising to the occasion when needed. One of those times would come soon.

Melvin Robinson, Copper John's 15-year-old sophomore center, hit for 12 a game, while forwards Billy Ray Fultz and Billy Ray Combs scored at just under 10 a game.

In spite of King Kelly Coleman's staggering individual numbers, Copper John had molded his boys into a pretty good team.

Betsy Lane came out and decided to play their game. They would run. It didn't work as Wayland won 92-84. Kelly scored 53.

Paintsville was next. What a season they had had, 28 and 2. Some observers thought this might be the end of the road for Wayland. Bryan Hall and Charles Hall were a solid one-two punch and were considered two of the better players in the region. "I talked to some of their players years later and they said when they watched us warm-up they knew they would beat us," Kelly said. "They said we looked like a rag-tag team."

Final score: Wayland 96, Paintsville 72.

Kelly scored 50.

Meanwhile, Pikeville had moved through their bracket, beating Sandy Hook and Flat Gap. It's worth noting that Flat Gap's Osborne scored 64 points in an earlier first round win over Morgan County.

It would be Wayland against Pikeville for the 15th Regional championship. The winner would advance to the Sweet 16 in Lexington.

Bob Daniels was a senior at Western Kentucky University. He had played at Oil Springs High School when he was a senior and Kelly was a freshman. Like everyone else he wanted to see the King play, and made the trip from Bowling Green for the final.

"There must have been at least 200 people outside the gym who couldn't get in," Daniels recalled. "It was a tough ticket."

Someone who didn't need a ticket that was inside the Pikeville gym that night was Adolph Rupp. He was there for one reason, to see one player play basketball.

Gordon Moore was also there. He covered mountain basketball for the *Courier-Journal* and he made it a point to be at all of the big games. And this was a big game. Moore has said that Rupp called Kelly the best high school player he had ever seen.

Many basketball experts across Kentucky felt like the Pikeville coach, John Bill Trivette was one of the best. His teams were always good. They were considered well coached and Trivette was one of the early day pioneers of the full court press. It was a rarity for teams in the 1950's to actually practice defense. Pikeville's press gave them a psychological advantage before a game even started. Combine this with a home crowd on their own court and Wayland, even with King Kelly Coleman, could be in over their heads tonight.

As good as John Bill Trivette's reputation was as a coach, such was not the case with Copper John Campbell. Copper John was the right coach in the right town, at the right time, for the right team, and for the right player. His teams were rumored to have had unorganized practices, with Copper John occasionally reading the newspaper, and even sipping "shine," while his boys played three-on-three or just shot around. As good as Kelly was, there was no way one player could beat Pikeville at Pikeville. Remember, Billy Ray Fultz and Billy Ray Combs had never played basketball before this season.

Regardless of how he did it or what method he used, Copper John was a motivator and coach, make no mistake about it.

Consider this: Of Wayland's five losses, three came in November and one in December. Hindman won 70-69, Betsy Lane 90-88 and Wheelwright 73-63, believe it or not all at Wayland. The December loss was at Central City. The rest of the year the only regular season defeat came late in the season at Carr Creek. That's pretty good coaching.

Gordon Moore wrote of the game: "Before a packed house with tense fans howling and hooting on every play, the great Coleman staged the greatest first half of his four years of high school net play. Unstoppable, he racked up 36 points in the first half to give his team a 54-45 halftime lead over Pikeville."

Although Wayland felt pretty good about their first half of play, Copper John was not very happy about the officiating. The King had three fouls as did center Melvin Robinson. Pikeville had picked up several fouls, but with their aggressive style of defense, it was expected. H.L. Justice fouled out with only 58 seconds gone in the third period. He had scored 10. Darwin Smith soon followed him to the bench after scoring 13. For the game Pikeville was led in scoring by Tommy Adkins with 22 and Howard Lockhart with 20.

Kelly, almost 50 years later said: "It was like Pikeville had their referee as we had ours."

That night Milford "Toodles" Wells and Humsey Yessin had been assigned to work the game, and Kelly has always felt Yessin was out to make sure Pikeville won the game. "He was good friends with the Dawahares in Pikeville," Kelly recalled in speaking about the family that owned several clothing stores throughout eastern Kentucky. "I was glad Toodles was there just to even it up."

Whether this was the case or not would probably depend on which team you were rooting for that night, but things would get interesting in the second half, very interesting.

The two officials would become almost as much a part of

the game as the players. Fifty-eight fouls were called, and 93 foul shots attempted in the game.

In the third quarter, with 1:29 remaining, for Wayland, the unthinkable happened. The King was whistled for his fifth foul. He had scored eight more in the third and 44 for the game, but he was done. Both teams had lost players in the third quarter.

There was well over a quarter to go, and although Wayland led, few believed they could hang on. Pikeville's fans were going wild, while Wayland's sat in stunned silence.

Wayland cheerleader Rebecca Hall couldn't bear to watch. She was back and forth from the sidelines to the rest room, just as she always did during close games.

The Wasps' Elmond Hall picked up where Kelly left off. He was scoring, but so was Pikeville. It was bedlam inside the packed gym. Copper John's cousin, Dog Campbell, the same guy that coached at Garrett, one of Waylands biggest rivals, was sitting directly behind the Wasps' bench that night. "Dog was doing everything he could that night to help Copper John," remembered Sherill Hall, one of Wayland's managers.

The Panthers had four starters on the bench from fouls, but sub Hooker Phillips was playing the game of this life. Wayland had a one point lead when Melvin Robinson picked up his fifth with 5:37 left in the game, but Hall kept shooting and hitting. With 39 seconds to go, Wayland was clinging to the lead at the free throw line, as Pikeville lost their sixth player to fouls and would finish the game with only four players on the court.

Elmond Hall finished the game with 25 points, 14 of them coming after Kelly fouled out. Fultz added 14 for the winners. Melvin Robinson remembers Hall's excitement in the last few minutes of the game. "Elmond kept hollering at

Copper John to put me and Kelly back in the game," Robinson remembers. "I don't know what he was thinking. We had already fouled out but he was telling coach to put us back in or we're gonna lose."

Copper John knew what he was doing and Wayland won 96-90 in what old-timers call the greatest 15th Regional finals ever played. He won a big one with Kelly on the bench. His coaching ability could no longer be questioned.

As for Elmond Hall, who played the greatest game of his life, his memories of that game almost 50 years later were simple. "I took us to state," he says.

The final box score told the story. Each team scored 33 field goals. Pikeville was whistled for 38 fouls to Wayland's 20. Pikeville hit 24 of 37 free shots while Wayland connected on 30 of 56. The six more made foul shots were the difference.

John Anthony Campbell, Copper John's son, was 9-years-old in 1956 and he remembers the excitement and tenseness that night, particularly after the game. "We had a state police escort out of there," recalls John Anthony. "Mom had the trophy in one hand and I was holding her other hand."

John Bill Trivette's son, Ken, remembers, "In 1986 we invited Kelly back to Pikeville for the 30th anniversary of that 1956 regional finals. The crowd gave him a 10 minute ovation. They loved him."

Chapter 11

W e've heard it all of our lives. "You'll only be remembered if you win, no one remembers who came in
second." Fifty years after Wayland High School
didn't win the 1956 Kentucky High School Basketball tournament, they are probably remembered more than the Carr
Creek team that did. The fact is Wayland didn't even finish
second. They finished third.

In 1956 a consolation game was played to determine the
third and fourth place teams, and it was this game that
solidified the reputation of Kelly Coleman.

Back then, newspaper reports were about the only means
of information being passed along from one end of the state
to the other. Television and radio were pretty much non-
existent when it came to sports reporting.

However, in 1955, when Kelly was a junior, word began
to spread about this scoring machine from the coal town of
Wayland, and by the time the tournament rolled around
the following year everyone knew about him.

That record setting state tournament performance by
Kelly and his teammates had never been seen before or since
and the consolation game made sure it would be a long time
before anyone who knows that a basketball is pumped and
not stuffed would forget it either.

The ride down to Lexington from Wayland was a real

King Kelly Coleman

trip back then. The Mountain Parkway hadn't been built yet and the curvy, two-lane roads, depending on weather conditions, could be quite treacherous.

It didn't pay to get in a hurry when driving the roads of eastern Kentucky.

Nevertheless, when Coach Copper John Campbell and high school principal, Lawrence B. Price met the players, team managers, cheerleaders, and a couple of other friends of the team, at the High School, the mood was that this was a team that was out to prove it was one of the elite teams in Kentucky. It didn't seem to matter that they were taking a four hour car ride, or that they had to borrow McDowell High School's warm ups. What did matter was that they were going to Lexington to win a state basketball championship. That had been Kelly's goal all year long after he returned to Wayland from Greenbrier Military School. Several cars were ready to go.

Copper John would be driving his 1954, four-door Chevrolet. With him in the front seat would be Mr. Price. Both would be making sure that all was well with their star player in the back seat, Kelly. They weren't about to let him out of their sight as long as Wayland had a game to play.

It was a little after 8 a.m., March 14 when the short line of cars pulled away from Wayland High School. They hoped to be in Lexington in time for lunch, check into the Phoenix Hotel, get a little rest and head over to Memorial Coliseum.

Most of Wayland had already left. They couldn't wait. Tickets weren't expected to be a problem. In past years the opening session was an easy ticket. It wasn't until the semis that tickets became a premium in the 12,000-seat building, so the Wayland fans wanted to make sure they had theirs.

Kelly remembered that day in March just before they left town. As is typical with many springs in Wayland, the rains came and the water rose. He lived up at Stampers

The Elk Horn Coal tipple in Wayland. Note the "wasp" logo that also became the mascot for Wayland High School

Early days of Wayland

Wayland's Methodist Church Parsonage-Superintendents house, 1938

Wayland, Kentucky

Left: Rusha Coleman

Below: United Mine Workers Officers, Elk Horn Coal Co. Guy Coleman is back row, 2nd from left.

Top right*: Guy, Rusha, Kelly, Sandra, Priscilla, Phillip, and Linda Carol Coleman*

Bottom left*: Rusha Coleman*

Bottom right*: Guy and Keith Coleman*

Top left: From right, Herbert Bentley, Kelly (age 11), and Bobby Doyle

Bottom left: Kelly (age 13) and Keith (age 2)

Bottom right: Kelly Coleman, May 1950

Kelly, age 13

Left: *Kelly, age 16*

Opposite: *Kelly, age 13, freshman year, 1952-53 season*

Kelly Coleman

Branch then, about a mile and a half from school. His dad was in Cleveland so Kelly had to walk to meet the team. The water in Wayland was so high that he had to make several detours in order to avoid it. The Fountain was flooded and several residents had to take boats from their homes to get to high ground so they could get to Lexington. A little flood wasn't going to rain on their parade.

The caravan arrived in Lexington none too soon for the players. They were hungry. Copper John wanted to make sure his boys were fed and then a little rest before heading over.

The lobby of the Phoenix was unlike anything the team from Wayland had ever seen. People were everywhere. Teams were checking in, coaches from across the state were visiting with each other, sportswriters were milling around, looking for a story. But the real buzz across the lobby and out on Main Street in front of the hotel was that fans were looking for tickets for the opening sessions.

King Kelly had arrived and he was the hottest ticket in town.

Late that afternoon as he and his teammates walked out of the Phoenix Hotel to head for the game, people were picking up leaflets that had been dropped from an airplane over the downtown area. As if everyone didn't already know, the leaflets proclaimed the arrival of King Kelly Coleman. And if Kelly didn't need more pressure, these pieces of paper swirling through the air quoted University of Kentucky Coach Adolph Rupp saying Kelly was the "greatest prep basketball player in history."

The leaflet was a story in itself. It was the brainchild of Gordon "Red" Moore, an insurance salesman from Prestonsburg. He was the same Gordon Moore who happened to also write about mountain basketball for the *Louisville Courier-Journal*.

Moore had been covering the regional tournament in Pikeville and Rupp was sitting next to him watching Kelly play. The legendary Kentucky coach told Moore and *Lexington Herald-Leader* sportswriter Billy Thompson that he had never seen anything like Coleman. He told Moore that more should be done to publicize this great player. Moore took Rupp's suggestion to heart. He printed 10,000 leaflets and rented an airplane for $250, and by Wednesday afternoon, the sky in downtown Lexington was full of King Kelly.

The leaflet listed Kelly's four year scoring record, reprinted a short story by Billy Thompson quoting Rupp calling Coleman the greatest prep player in history. Then there was a five line story by Moore under the headline: "Coleman has the agility of a 120-pounder." It seemed a bit out of place and would only add to the pressure on Coleman. Some observers felt years later that the flyer created more hostility toward Kelly than it did in actually publicizing him.

Moore's story read as follows: "Kelly Coleman is the biggest discovery on the mountains of Kentucky since coal was found 50 years ago. He is not only a prolific scorer but a terrific rebounder, dribbler, and all around team man. He never shoots when another teammate is open, and he has the uncanny knack of following his own and teammate's shots for two-pointers. Once the ball is on the offensive board, he keeps it in the air, never once bringing it down as most high school players do, until it goes in."

A single line at the bottom of the leaflet read: Courtesy: REDMORE INSURANCE AGENCY AND PRESTONSBURG, KENTUCKY FANS. It would be a load for any basketball player to live up to, much less a 17-year-old from Wayland.

Kelly paid little attention to it. He had only one thing on his mind, and that was beating Shelbyville, their first round opponent.

Chapter 12

When Copper John and his team arrived at Memorial Coliseum for their first round game against Shelbyville he did his best to keep his boys calm, relying on his personal experiences of playing in the Sweet 16 for Hindman back in 1939 when he was the leading scorer in the championship game, and then as a coach, taking the Wasps to the big show in 1947 and 1951.

Most of the boys had never been to a city as big as Lexington, or stayed in a hotel as large as the Phoenix. If it hadn't been for the trip to Central City back in late December, this would have been their longest trip from home.

Still, nothing Copper John could say or do prepared his team for their initial reaction when they walked inside of Memorial Coliseum. "It was so big," Kelly recalled. "It looks like two goals sitting in a cornfield. We were used to playing our games in a little gym with the goals hanging from the end walls."

Those 12,000 seats were rapidly filling, as many fans wanted to get there early to make sure they saw the King warm up. Many crowded around the Wayland end of the floor making sure they got a good look. Kelly knew they were there to see him.

He felt an excitement. It was something special. He had thought about the Sweet 16 for a long time. His mind flashed back to the hard fought win over Pikeville and how close it all came to ending there. He fouled out in the third quarter of that game, so it had been several days since he had played in game conditions.

The place was packed and Kelly could see people standing in the corners of the Coliseum and even in the upper aisles. Every shot he took, now, even in warm-ups, were being critiqued by every one in the house.

Wayland and Shelbyville concluded their pre-game shots and returned to the bench for team introductions. Seniors Billy Ray Combs and Billy Ray Fultz were introduced at the forward position. Sophomore Melvin Robinson at center; and seniors Elmond Hall at one guard and Kelly Coleman at the other. The public address announcer didn't mention the word "King." He didn't have to.

Kelly jumped center, just as he had done in every game previously. And, as he has done in almost every game before, he controlled the tip. But what happened next he was not prepared for, and it would stay with him, changing the way he felt about basketball forever.

The tip went to Billy Ray Combs who quickly passed it back to Kelly. As soon as it was in his hands it started. By now there were over 13,000 people in the gym, and to Kelly it sounded like every one of them was booing him. A routine developed. Every time he had the ball they booed. When he passed it the booing stopped.

He was stunned. He couldn't figure it out. He had done nothing to those people. It seemed like everyone was looking for a weakness in his game. He was just a kid from the mountains who could play basketball better than anyone else in Kentucky and he was having to put up with this.

Kelly asked himself, "Why?"

For the first time ever the opening session of the state tournament had been a sellout. Those 12,000 seats turned into more than 13,000. There was only one reason, King Kelly Coleman. He wasn't just on the sports page he was front page.Perhaps people resented the publicity. He hadn't asked for it. Neither did he ask for those leaflets to be dropped from the sky. He hadn't asked to be called a king. All he wanted to do was play basketball and win a state championship for Wayland.

Although it may have seemed like 13,000 rooting against Kelly, that wasn't the case. Hundreds from Wayland and neighboring mountain towns had made the trip to see and pull for Kelly and fellow mountain schools Carr Creek and Bell County. Many even carried balloons on a string with one word on it, "Coleman." Also to be factored in was that Kelly had made it known that his college choice was not going to be the beloved Kentucky Wildcats but instead the West Virginia Mountaineers in Morgantown. This didn't sit well with many in the crowd who loved their Kentucky Wildcats.

In spite of everything going on inside of Kelly's head, and with the crowds involvement, he still managed to score 50 points as Wayland beat Shelbyville 87-76.

For Kelly, after that, the game wasn't fun anymore. It had lost some of its innocence. He was turned off to some of the people in Kentucky. They had judged him without knowing him. The game became less important, more of a job.

Nevertheless, Kelly and his teammates were able to gather themselves to play Earlington, a 63-57 winner over Monticello in their opener. Once again the session was a sellout. Earlington's star player was 6'-8" All-State sophomore Harry Todd. Todd possessed a big sweeping hook shot, not seen at the state tournament since Doodle Floyd helped lead Cuba to the 1952 title.

The game was close. Earlington led 36-28 at the half. Todd had scored 22 first half points to Kelly's 20, but the second half would belong to the Wasps. Kelly added 19 more to finish with 39, while Todd managed but six more to total 28.

Meanwhile, Carr Creek had advanced to the semi-finals with a 70-68 opening round win over powerhouse Central City and Corky Withrow. Senior Freddie Maggard hit a last second shot to move the Creekers into the quarter-finals, where they easily defeated Allen County 69-45.

WAYLAND'S
"KING KELLY" COLEMAN
Is In Town
FOUR YEAR RECORD TO DATE

Year	Games	Total	Average
1955-56	37	1734 *	46.8
1954-55	36	1174 *	32.6
1953-54	30	784	26.1
1952-53	20	386	19.3
	123	4078	33.2

* STATE RECORD

Kelly Coleman Is Called Greatest Prep Basketeer In History By Adolph Rupp

By Billy Thompson (Lexington Herald-Leader)

"The greatest high school player who ever lived . . . A combination of Cliff Hagan, Frank Ramsey and all the other great stars who have played at Kentucky."

The quotes are from Adolph Rupp, veteran University of Kentucky basketball coach.

And the player to whom he is referring is Kelly Coleman, the crackerjack cager at Wayland.

Rupp, who has been watching basketeers for 15 these many years journed to Pikeville Friday night to see the heralded Wasp warrior in action.

"He is fantastic. You have to see this boy to believe what he can do —and I still am not sure I believe it.

"He can shoot any sort of a shot. Mostly, though, he fires one-handers from the head of the circle.

"He dribbbles behind his back as good as any player I have ever seen. He came down the floor in the second quarter last night, dribbled behind his back and the ball was stolen from him. A few minutes later, he did the same thing, faked his opponent out of his shoes and hit the nicest shot I have ever seen, ly and isn't too good defensively, but he sure knows what a basketball is for.

"He resembles Frank Ramsey coming down the floor. He is big (6-3 and weighs 212) and his shots don't hit the rim and roll in. They are dead center. The net swishes upward as the ball glides through.

"He can do more with a basketball than Cliff Hagan, and that is saying a lot," Rupp added.

(Both Hagan and Ramsey were All-Americas at Kentucky).

COLEMAN HAS THE AGILITY OF A 120-POUNDER
By Gordon Moore (Louisville Courier-Journal)

Kelly Coleman is the biggest discovery in the mountains of Kentucky since coal was found 50 years ago. He is not only a prolific scorer but a terrific rebounder, dribbler, and all around team-man. He never shoots when another teammate is open, and he has the uncanny knack of following his own and teammates' shots for two-pointers. Once the ball is on the offensive board, he keeps it in the air, never once bringing it down as most high school players do, until it goes in.

Courtesy: REDMORE INSURANCE AGENCY AND PRESTONSBURG, KENTUCKY FANS

Chapter 13

Wayland and Carr Creek had split during the regular season. The lobby of the Phoenix was more like a circus than a hotel. Everyone was looking for tickets and it seemed like everyone was looking for Kelly. The Carr Creek-Wayland game was being talked about as much as any other game at the state tournament in years. Some even said tickets were selling for more than their printed price.

Kelly was nowhere to be seen. Copper John Campbell and Lawrence B. Price made sure of that. They made sure Kelly wasn't distracted by all of the glad-handlers, or maybe some of the gamblers, and for sure some of the well-meaning girls at the state tournament. The only time his teammates saw him was at team meals and the game. The rest of the time Kelly was pretty much under lock and key. Or so they thought.

Lexington could have been a foreign country as far as the Wayland boys and cheerleaders were concerned. They would stroll the downtown sidewalks together, just looking. They were proud of their school jackets and just as proud when fans and students from other schools would stop and talk, even if much of the talk was about Kelly.

For seniors Billy Ray Combs, Billy Ray Fultz, Elmond Hall, Jackie Thornberry and James Vernon Hall, they knew this would probably be the last time they would play for an organized team. A couple of the boys entertained the throught of going to college and maybe even making the basketball team. But reality told them they would graduate from Wayland, find a job and get married.

None of them ever wanted to work in the mines. Sophomore Melvin Robinson had a future in basketball and Curtis Ray Slone was just a freshman.

Wayland's three cheerleaders were having the time of their lives. Senior Maude Hatcher's mother was the chaperon and Mrs. Hatcher was glad they would all be staying in one hotel room. It would make her job easier. Not that Sylvia Reed and Rebecca Hall were problems, mind you. It's just that, well, they were kids. They loved looking in the store windows, talking to other cheerleaders, and they were oh so proud to be from Wayland. They smiled all the time, not because it was expected, but because they were happy.

Even with Maude's mother in the room most of the time, the girls were creative in their fun. They had received tickets to all of the tournament games, but there was no way they would spend all of their time watching basketball games when the Wasps weren't playing, and besides they had discovered Ruth Hunt Candy. With the demand for tickets greater than the available supply, Sylvia Reed took the others tickets to the lobby to sell. She came back with money and the three girls went looking for candy.

Copper John made sure his boys weren't near the cheerleaders. They needed to keep their thoughts on basketball. But boys will be boys and girls will be girls and soon they figured out a way to communicate.

Melvin Robinson's room was just above the cheerleaders and when Maude's mom left the room, the girls would call up and Melvin would lower a beer down to them. It was high school kids just being kids. Nothing more.

Chapter 14

Kelly had been kept under wraps for a reason other than gamblers, sportswriters, an occasional beer and girls. He had the flu.

The win over Pikeville in the regional finals had been played out other than just on the basketball court. Kelly said the water in the locker room showers had been cut off and the team left the gym quickly while still wet with sweat. As a result he caught a cold, his throat hurting and his body aching. He hadn't been able to shake it, and that was one of the big reasons he wasn't seen hanging out in the lobby or window shopping on Main Street. The Lexington March air was cold.

Inside Memorial Coliseum, however, it was hot. It was a full house in anticipation of the "game-of-the-tournament" to this point.

Wayland had defeated Carr Creek 70-68 early in the regular season and the Indians returned the favor with a 79-74 win in the season finale. Most observers picked the winner of this game to win it all.

Carr Creek had a great all-around team, with two players, Bobby Shepherd at center, and E.A. Couch at guard being named All-State. Then there was Freddie Maggard, Warren Amburgey and Jim Cahoun. Although they were probably a better balanced team than any other in the tourney, they had no one who could match Kelly.

Carr Creek Coach Morton Combs wasn't sure what his game plans would be. Copper John, on the other hand, knew exactly what his would be. Kelly had to look for his shot, Elmond Hall had to be ready to take charge if they double or triple teamed Kelly. Forward Billy Ray Fultz, usually solid as a rock on defense, would not be a factor. He had not recovered from an ankle injury suffered in the Earlington game, and James Vernon Hall would be taking his place. Melvin Robinson would have to step up against the strong inside game of Shepherd. If Shepherd and Couch were able to get their 24-point average, the Wasps would be in big trouble.

But big trouble is exactly what Coach Combs expected from King Kelly, sick or not. He'd heard these stories before, and the great Carr Creek coach wasn't about to let his guard down now.

Carr Creek would be very popular with the sellout crowd. Their legendary 1928 team that lost a four overtime final to Ashland, was still talked about in high school basketball circles.

It was no secret that Carr Creek had three, maybe four players who were being recruited by big time schools to further their basketball careers. Wayland had one.

Shepherd was considering the University of Kentucky, where it was rumored he might even like to tryout for the football team, even though he had no high school experience. Dayton and West Virginia wanted both Shepherd and Couch to play for them. The rest of the Indians would also have a chance to play some more after their prep careers were over.

Coach Combs, right up to game time, wasn't sure how he would handle Kelly. At least that's what he told the press.

In the previous games between the two teams Warren Amburgey had guarded Kelly, and although he didn't exactly shut him down he did hold him under his season average. Kelly scored 44 and 40. If anyone held King Kelly Coleman under his scoring average in 1956, it no doubt gave him some sort of bragging rights.

Kelly had become a celebrity for sure. Writers who weren't even sportswriters were writing about him, and Adolph Rupp had told Copper John that Kelly was a combination of Alex Groza, Frank Ramsey and Cliff Hagan. Pretty heavy stuff for a 17-year-old to carry around. Copper John said, "It made him feel his Cheerios, if you know what I mean."

As good as Kelly was, there were doubters, those out there that were looking for flaws. They talked about his shot not being perfect, he was not a great jumper, he was overweight and out of shape, and he couldn't play a lick of defense. Copper John had his own take on Kelly's defense. "I'd be foolish to let him guard the opposing team's best player, he's more valuable on offense. Why would I want him to pick up two or three quick fouls and be on the bench with me?"

It has always been intriguing to Kelly that people put the label on him as being fat, overweight and out of shape. "When I was at Wayland I wore a size 32 basketball shorts," he recalled. "Maybe it was because I was big chested, and my jersey would come out over my waist."

As for being out of shape Kelly had this to say: "Our team averaged 91 points and I averaged 47. A lot of those points coming in the fourth quarter, so if I were out of shape how could this have happened."

And what about his lack of jumping ability?

"Copper John told me I controlled 90 percent of the center jumps and jump balls I was involved in. I had a technique of leaning into the other player just enough to throw him off a bit. As for rebounding just look at my numbers. I may have been one of the top rebounders in the history of the state."

For the most part schools didn't keep rebounding stats, at least on a regular basis, back then, but Kelly says he knows he got at least 25 rebounds every night out.

Kelly's dad, Guy, was ready to see his son play for the first time since his freshman year. Now living in Cleveland and working at a steel mill, the elder Coleman left for Lexington by plane. Kelly would be glad to see him and even happier that he would get to see him play in the state tournament. The weather, however, is one thing no one could control, not even Kelly. Dangerous weather conditions prevented Guy's plane from landing at Blue Grass Field. That disappointment further affected Kelly's experience in Lexington.

Chapter 15

Wayland and Carr Creek were on the floor. The winner would play for the state championship against the winner of the Henderson-Bell County game. The two losers would meet in consolidation game to determine third and fourth. None of these teams wanted to play in that game. It was for losers.

Three of the teams left standing were from the mountains, and the other, Henderson, was from the far western part of the state. Gone were the two big city schools. In the first round, Henderson defeated the largest school in the state, Louisville Valley, 80-62; and Bell County took care of Lexington Lafayette in the quarters by a 65-63 margin in two overtimes. Lafayette was one of the early favorites and their star Billy Ray Lickert was pretty good. Coach Ralph Carlisle and his Generals would have to wait till next year.

Ted Sanford, Commissioner of the Kentucky High School Athletic Association was delighted that Wayland and Kelly were in the tournament, because, as he said, "It relieves my staff of worrying about selling tickets. They want to see Kelly play and when he is on the schedule we run out of tickets early and can concentrate on other things."

The press loved Kelly as well. When it was all over, the *Louisville Courier-Journal* and the *Lexington Herald-Leader*, combined to publish Kelly's picture 29 times and printed his name 141 times during the four-day state tournament.

Copper John knew that Kelly hadn't played his best. Even though he and principal Lawrence Price were doing everything in their power to control Kelly's surroundings away from the court, they had little, if any, influence over the hostile crowds that had greeted Kelly up until this point.

Copper John told the media after the win over Earlington, "I'm hoping he comes through against Carr Creek. He has been so bewildered by the reception he has had here that he can't keep his mind on the game."

In the meantime Coach Morton Combs said he might concentrate on stopping Coleman's teammates. "You just knock yourself out trying to defense Coleman," he said. "And I might just let him go on and get his 40 or 50. If you fool around with him, you have two or three of your regulars fouled out and it ruins your own offense."

As the two teams went through their warm-up paces there was no need to even glance down at the other end of the court. There was no need to check each other out. After all, five of the Wasps actually lived in Knott County, the same county Carr Creek hails from. This game was neighbor against neighbor, with a lot at stake.

The referees that day were Dick Betz and Dero Downing. Downing would later become president of Western Kentucky University, but decades later he remembered Kelly and the game as if it were played yesterday.

"He had a jump shot that leaned into the defender," Downing said. "And I called a couple of fairly early first half offensive fouls on him. He was so big and strong that he could wipe out a defender when he shot. I remember the Wayland people getting on me pretty good."

Downing, who had played for Ed Diddle at Western and officiated in the Southeastern and Ohio Valley Conferences for several years, had seen some good basketball players, and says that Coleman was the best scorer he has ever seen play the game. "When Kelly Coleman crossed the mid-court line he was in position to score. He was a machine," Downing said.

The two early fouls on Kelly combined with Coach Comb's strategy to put Jim Calhoun on the Wayland ace had, for the most part, taken Kelly out of his game.

Elmond Hall, the Wasps unsung hero in the regional final win over Pikeville, however, picked up the slack. With Kelly getting only one first quarter field goal and four out of five free throws, Hall scored 12 points to give Wayland a 20-15 lead.

The score didn't bother Carr Creek. Coach Combs was content to keep the score low and prevent Kelly from getting into a rhythm. He would continue to double and triple team him periodically.

The second quarter was much the same. No one was tearing it up for either team. Bobby Shepherd, who managed only two free throws in the first quarter for Carr Creek, picked up eight second quarter points, and one of the state's best, E.A. Couch, had only four first half points to go along with Freddie Maggard's six.

If you looked only at Carr Creeks stats you would have thought they would have been in big trouble. Not so.

In the second quarter, Kelly scored only one basket from the field and was four of four from the line. Hall added two baskets and Melvin Robinson for the half had a field goal and two free throws. The 12 second quarter points for Wayland were a season low. No one could remember the last time a Copper John Campbell team had scored only 12 points in a quarter. And for sure no one could remember when the great King Kelly Coleman had made only two field goals in a half. Perhaps you would have to go all the way back to his sophomore year when he drank that tequila before one of the games. This time there was no tequila. It was very simple. In basketball it's difficult to score without the ball.

Wayland led 32-28 at the half and Morton Combs was pleased at the position his Carr Creek team was in. Elmond Hall had scored 16 points to lead Wayland and Bobby Shepherd had 10 for Carr Creek.

The second half saw Carr Creek put a little more zip in their offense as they outscored the Wasp 20-15 to take a 48-42 lead.

Couch and Shepherd each hit four baskets in the third, while Maggard added one to round out the Carr Creek scoring.

For Wayland, what offense they could muster came off eight points from Hall and six from Kelly. Robinson added a free throw. Kelly could show only five field baskets and eight free shots for three quarters of work. Many other players would be satisfied with 18 points at this stage. There had been many games where he had scored that many in one quarter. Nevertheless, he was going to the boards in his typical style, hard and often.

It was still anybody's game. Everyone in Memorial Coliseum knew it was only a matter of time before the great Coleman would break loose.

Coleman did not score in the first two minutes of the fourth quarter, but then he became the King Kelly of old, hitting five baskets in the last six minutes.

With 1:41 left Carr Creek led 63-62. A free throw by Couch made it 64-62. Then with 43 seconds left, Shepherd tipped in a missed shot to put Carr Creek up 66-62. It looked like it was over and Wayland was in big trouble.

Coleman answered with a basket, and Hall added a free throw to cut the Carr Creek lead to 66-65. After a change of possession with 18 seconds remaining Melvin Robinson got loose under the basket to score. Wayland led 67-66. No one in the building was sitting.

Carr Creek took a time out and the plan Coach Combs laid out was for the ball to go inside to Shepherd. He was the Indians go-to-guy all season, so why change now.

On the other end of the floor, Copper John was telling his boys not to give up anything easy. Don't let Shepherd get a lay-up inside. If they get a shot make them earn it - - from the outside.

Carr Creek inbounded the ball, and here they came. For Carr Creek the seconds were ticking off way too fast. For Wayland it was like the clock was in slow motion.

Freddie Maggard had the ball. The clock was under 10. He looked for Shepherd down low, just as he was told. And just as Copper John had instructed his boys, they had packed the defense in tight around Shepherd. For sure there would be no cheapies. If the Indians got a shot it would be from outside.

Maggard dribbled slightly to the left and quickly back to the right just beyond the top of the key. He now had no choice. He would take the final shot.

When Maggard jumped into the air as the ball left his hand, the clock showed five seconds. All ten players, the two officials, time keeper Big Six Henderson, official scorer J.W. Trapp, and the however many thousands of fans who had jammed their way into the game, were focused only on one thing - - the basket.

Maggard's shot sliced through the net at the three second mark. The game was over and for the second time in the tournament, Maggard had hit a game winner. It was his only basket of the quarter.

Carr Creek 68, Wayland 67.

"It was 22, 23 feet out," Maggard said years later of his

game-winner against Wayland. "It would easily have been a three-pointer today."

Maggard says that both teams had such great respect for each other over the years. "We knew we would get their best and they knew we would give ours," he said. "I'd seen over the years Kelly probably average 45 against us except for that one state tournament game. "Coach Combs told Jim Calhoun before the game to follow Kelly everywhere he goes, even to the restroom if he goes."

Maggard says that Carr Creek knew Kelly's style of play and habits. Playing against him so many times over the years they had noticed things."If you were guarding him and he shot and then broke for the basket, you knew he had missed," he said. "But if he shot and turned around you knew you could forget it."

In winning, Carr Creek had put four players in double figures, led by Shepherd's 26 and Couch's 17. Calhoun, playing well at both ends of the floor hit for 11, and Maggard added 10. Warren Amburgey, the Indians other starter went scoreless from the field but hit two big three throws in the fourth quarter. Ed Richardson came off the bench in last period to hit one basket.

Fifty-eight of Waylands 67 points came from Coleman and Hall. Robinson added seven and the only other two points came on a fourth quarter basket from guard Billy Ray Combs. Billy Ray Fultz, still hobbling from an opening game ankle sprain, was scoreless.

Many so called basketball know-it-alls felt like for all practical purposes this was the championship game. Forget the fact that T.L. Plain's Henderson team had played their way into the championship game with a 68-63 win over Bell County. Maybe they were right. Later that night Carr Creek took the title game 72-68 over Henderson.

Kelly did manage 28 rebounds to go along with his 28 points. And although it was, by the Kings standards, a very pedestrian type game, his rebounding numbers still stand as a single game state tournament record.

Almost 50 years later at the age of 92, Morton Combs, had vivid memories of Kelly Coleman and his Wayland teammates. Sitting in the den of his home next to Carr Creek High School overlooking beautiful Carr Creek Reservoir, Coach Combs had this to say: "I felt like the three best teams in the state were in the same bracket. Us, Central City and Wayland were put together and I thought we were the only team that could beat Wayland, because we had just done it in our last game of the season.

"Wayland wasn't just a one man team. The Hall and Robinson boys were good," he said. "And Kelly was a good all-around player. He could play at both ends. His game was all about timing. He was always in the right place at the right time.

"I've been asked many times who is the best player I've ever seen? I can honestly say I've never seen anybody better than Kelly. I saw Jerry West and he wasn't any better than Kelly.

"I always wished I could have coached him."

In his book about the 1956 Carr Creek team, *The Overtime Kids*, author Don Miller wrote: "The state champ that year was Carr Creek, but the tournament always will belong to King Kelly."

Chapter 16

Consolation games are for losers, and that was the game facing Wayland and Bell County. Both teams had only a few hours before they played each other, and for what?

For Kelly the loss to Carr Creek was devastating. Burning deep inside of his sometime nonchalant attitude was a fire to succeed that only few athletes have.

Sitting on the concrete floor in the Memorial Coliseum locker room, Kelly was quiet, but visibly shaken. The loss was a great part of it, but so was the way he was still being treated by crowds. The boos and jeers, although diminished from the two earlier games, were still evident.

Most sportswriters across the state still get their digs in on Kelly, but there was one who Kelly felt like he could trust - - Billy Thompson.

Thompson had covered Kelly for the last two years, and the Wayland star felt like he had been treated fairly by the *Herald-Leader* writer. So when Thompson entered the Wasps locker room that afternoon, Kelly was ready to talk.

"You're the only writer whose stood by me," Coleman said in a voice choked with emotion. "You tell em' Billy, tell em' I'm going to give em' the greatest basketball game they've ever seen. I'm going to get 60, and then, Billy, you tell em' to drop dead."

It was reported in some circles that Kelly actually told Thompson to "tell em' to kiss my ass." Thompson couldn't and wouldn't print that.

To the surprise of some in the Wayland locker room that day, Pikeville coach, John Bill Trivette came in to console Copper John Campbell and Kelly. Even though it was Wayland who kept his team from being in Lexington, Trivette was very upset with what they had seen and heard from the fans.

"Kelly, those people want your blood," he said of the crowd. All of a sudden in Kelly's mind, this game with Bell County would be more than just a game for losers. It would now be all about going out as a winner.

Carr Creek's Freddie Maggard had his memories of what to expect from Kelly in that consolation game.

"Our rooms were right across the hall from Wayland's," Maggard remembered." I saw Kelly in the hall as they were leaving for the game and he said to all of us that "these people are getting ready to see what I can really do."

From the outset everyone knew it was going to be an up and down game. Bell County was pretty good and they felt like they could run with Wayland, and to coach Willie Hendrickson's credit he was not going to disappoint the full house on hand to see a game for losers – the consolation game.

Bell County had a couple of pretty fair guards in John Mayes and John Brock. Although both were well under six feet, they were quick and could score. Inside they had a 6'4" center, Jack Johnson, who was being looked at by some of the smaller colleges. Bruce Miracle and Murph Slusher rounded out the starters.

Brock was excited that Coach Hendrickson had given him the responsibility of guarding Coleman. Brock's older brother, Al, had told him there would be a $5 bonus if he could hold the state's all-time leader to under 25.

Word spread among the Bell County fans and the re-ward to Brock was up to $25.

Brock was pumped. He even told some that he was "go-ing to hold him under 10 points." But four minutes into the game Kelly registered his eleventh point to break the single tournament scoring record set by Hazard's Johnny Cox the previous year. Brock still had a crack at the 25 number. But at halftime the game was pretty much over. Wayland led 72-43 and King Kelly had 38 of those.

Brock recalled that at halftime his coach changed up the defense to shut Kelly down.

"He told us that we weren't going to let Coleman set any records against us," remembered Brock. "He told John Mayes and I to get all over him when he had the ball out front and if he went down under the basket Jack Johnson would take him, and Mayes and I would collapse down and help him out.

Kelly came out of the locker room firing. He remem-bered everything he shot went in, or at least it seemed. Something was happening among the fans, too. No longer were there the ugly taunts, but now it had turned into ap-plause when Kelly scored. They were caught up in the ex-citement of both teams racing up and down the floor at break-neck speed scoring, scoring and scoring some more. Forget the fact that very little defense was being played. Scoring points was what this game was all about.

When Copper John finally took Kelly out of the game there was a little less than two minutes to go and his star had hammered in 27 of 52 field goal attempts and 14 of 18 free throws for 68 points. Melvin Robinson added 22, Hall 19 and Combs 11. Johnson led Bell County with 32.

The transformation of the crowd had come full circle. They were now on their feet, cheering wildly, finally giving King Kelly his dues. But it was too late.

Copper John said Kelly could have scored 90 or even 100, but he asked the other boys to play it straight and not concentrate on his total points.

Brock agreed. "He could have scored no telling how many. And back then the clock kept running when the ball went out of bounds. It stopped only on free throws. He probably lost at least two or three minutes a game. Then if you add the three point line, oh boy."

Ernie Sparkman, a long time Hazard radio station owner, who played for Rupp at UK in the 1940's remembers seeing Kelly play. "There were a lot of things you could say about him as a player," he offers. "But the one thing I remember is that he made the game look so easy. There was no wasted motion. It may have looked like he was loafing. He only moved when he thought he could accomplish something, or when it counted. Everybody else was running up and down the floor wearing themselves out and beating themselves to death."

When the final horn sounded Wayland and Kelly had made history with their 122-89 win.

Wayland fans raced onto the court, with several of them hoisting Kelly on their shoulders. The picture is there. A sweat-soaked #66 riding the shoulders of friends. There a slight smile across his face probably because of his surprise of how quickly they were able to lift him up. Kelly would later say he didn't want to be paraded around the floor, but that he went along with it because the game also belonged to Wayland fans and all of the others from the mountains who had pulled for him.

But not everyone saw the game, or its final score as a good thing. Almost 50 years later, sportswriter Earl Cox said that game, more than any other, did more to lead to the demise of the consolation game.

"It was a farce," Cox says, "Absolutely no defense at all."

With that said, had it not been for the consolation game

in 1956, the fans of Kentucky basketball in general would have been the real losers, not just those in attendance that March 17th afternoon in Lexington.

Earl Ruby, Sports Editor *Courier-Journal*, wrote that it was Kelly Coleman's performance and ability to draw a crowd that led the State Tournament to move to Freedom Hall in Louisville.

Think about this. In one tournament, four games, Kelly Coleman became the most legendary player to ever perform at the Boys Sweet 16.

Several players made multiple appearances at the Big Show. Richie Farmer played in five with Clay County. Eleven others played in four, among those Wah Wah Jones, Linville Puckett, J.R. VanHoose, and Kenny Higgs. And then there has been Ralph Beard, Cliff Hagan, Frank Ramsey, Frank Selvy, Howie Crittenden, Doodle Floyd, Kenny Kuhn, Johnny Cox, Vernon Hatton, Corky Withrow, Harry Todd, Ralph Richardson, Bobby Rascoe, Billy Ray Lickert, Julius Berry, Tom Thacker, Randy Embry, Larry Conley, Mike Silliman, Clem Haskins, Wes Unseld, Dwight Smith, Butch Beard, Mike Casey, Jim McDaniels, Ron King, Robert Brooks, Jack Givens, Darrell Griffith, Jeff Lamp, Dirk Minniefield, Manual Forrest, Todd May, Paul Andrews, Steve Miller, Rex Chapman, John Pelphrey, Allan Houston, Travis Ford, DeJuan Wheat, Scott Hundley and Chris Lofton to name a few of the great ones. But none left the footprint that King Kelly Coleman did. Not one of them.

NOT
PICTURED

NOT
PICTURED

Seniors

FIRST ROW: Jacqueline Manns, Ethel Hall, Betty Hopkins.

SECOND ROW: (not shown) Kelly Coleman, Elizabeth Wolfe,

(not shown) Bill Fultz.

CLASS FLOWER: Pink and White Carnations

CLASS COLORS: Pink and White

CLASS SONG: "I Believe"

CLASS MOTTO: "No Wind Does Him Good,
Who Steers For No Port"

*Kelly Coleman's senior picture, or rather, where it should've been; from the
1956 Floyd County yearbook, the Wayland High School pages.*

A yearbook display of the 1956 varsity Wayland Wasps

Basketball

BILLY R. COMBS

AFTON BATES

BOBBY BENTLEY

RAY SLONE

Varsity A

Mr. L.B. Price - Cheerleaders - Coach J. Campbell   Managers

A yearbook display of the 1956 varsity Wayland Wasps

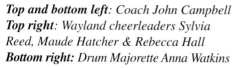

Top and bottom left*: Coach John Campbell*
Top right*: Wayland cheerleaders Sylvia*
Reed, Maude Hatcher & Rebecca Hall
Bottom right: *Drum Majorette Anna Watkins*

Top, From left to right: *Kelly Coleman, Maude Hatcher, Elmond Hall, Becky Hall, Melvin Robinson, Billy Ray Combs, Jackie Thornsberry*

1956 Wayland Wasps

Top right: '56 team
with coach Copper
John Campbell

Bottom: Kelly Coleman
at the McDowell
tournament in 1956

Top left: Coach Copper John Campbell in front of Wayland H.S.

BATTLE GRAHAM TONIGHT—Wayland's Wasps, who meet Graham's Hawks in the opening game of the Central City Invitational tonight, are (from left, front) cheerleaders Sylvia Reed, Maude Ellen Hatcher and Rebecca Hall. Second row: manager Jackie Collins, Melvin Robinson, Billy Ray Fultz, Kelly Coleman, Elmond Hall, James V. Hall, manager Sherril Hall. Back row: Principal L. B. Price, Curtis Ray Slone, Jackie Thronberry, Afton Bates, Ray Alton Slone, Bill Ray Combs and Coach "Copper" John Campbell. Central City will play Elkton in the second game tonight.

Wayland Players Lean on Their Weary Star

Even after the victory over Shelbyville, Wayland players depended on their star—Kelly Coleman. They lean on the weary King, who scored 50 points, while waiting for the Memorial Coliseum locker-room to be opened. Left to right are Billy Combs, Bobby Bentley, Jackie Thornberry, Coleman, Elwood Hall, Billy Fultz and James Hall. Beads of perspiration cover Coleman's face.

March 19, 1956, Coleman shoots a free-throw

Top left: Earlington's all-state Harry Todd fouls Kelly in a 1956 state tournament game

Bottom: Kelly in a 1956 state tournament game against Earlington

MAT MAN AGAIN — Kelly Coleman drives for the basket as Earlington's Ronald Robinson (22) and Donald Fugate (88) attempt to stop him.

Bottom: *Kelly blocked out by Warren G. Amburgey of Carr Creek*

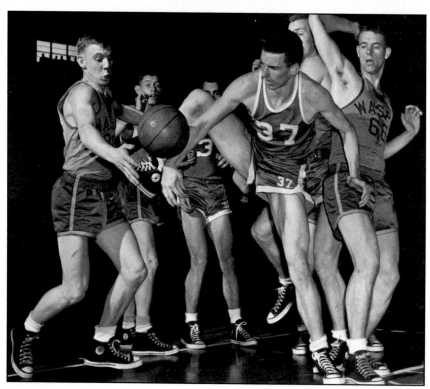

HERE'S KELLY! . . . But if Kelly's "shy-ness" kept him off the floor during presentation cere-monies is doesn't show in this locker room shot during a visit by former University of Kentucky All-American Frank Ramsey (left). Coleman scored 68 points in the tourney consolation game against Bell County.

Kelly at the 1956 state tournament with U.K. All-American Bob Burrow

Kelly drives in for a layup against Bell County in the 1956 state tournament consolation game

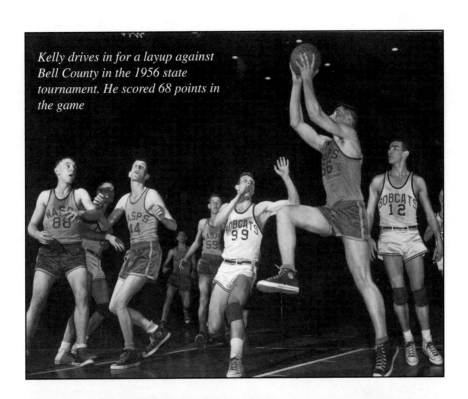

Kelly drives in for a layup against Bell County in the 1956 state tournament. He scored 68 points in the game

Players watch as Coleman's shot breaks the scoring record

From Sunday's Late Editions   Associated Press Wirephoto

'KING KELLY' COLEMAN, Wayland High School basketball star, is carried from the floor by his admirers after scoring a record-smashing 68 points last night as the Wasps beat Bell County, 122 to 89, in the consolation game at the state tournament.

Bell County Coach Willie Hendrickson, Kelly Coleman, and Coach John Campbell

The Windup of A Big Basketball Weekend

WHERE'S KELLY? . . . Here is the Kentucky State High School All-Tournament team. Well, almost, that is. Conspicuous by his absence (and by his attractive sister who subbed for him) is Wayland's Kelly Coleman whose four-game total of 185 points shattered several tourney records. Linda Carol Coleman (circled) explained that Kelly was "too shy" to face the crowd and receive his trophy. The team: (kneeling, left to right) Rex Story, Mayfield; Dave Eakins, Henderson; E. A. Couch and Bobby Shepherd, Carr Creek, and Pascal Benson, Henderson. Standing (from left) are Harry Todd, Earlington; Byron Pinson, Henderson; Linda Carol Coleman, Wayland; Corky Withrow, Central City, and Billy Lickert, Lafayette.

March 31, 1956, Sen. Doug Hays presents an award to Kelly Coleman

Sign donated to Wayland after the 1956 season. It still hangs in the Wayland gym
Previous page, top left: *March 1956, Coleman in dressing room after scoring 68 points*
Previous page, top right: *Linda Carol Coleman, Kelly's 15 year old sister, accepting tha All-Tourney trophy from Ted Sanford, Commissioner KHSAA*

Floyd County To Pay Honor To Wayland Cagers Tonight

By GORDON MOORE
Courier-Journal Correspondent

Wayland, Ky., March 28.— Civic clubs of Wayland, Lackey and Garret will reward the 1955-56 Wayland High School basketball team with an elaborate banquet in the school's gymnasium here tomorrow night.

Principal speakers will be Bernie Shively, athletic director at the University of Kentucky; Billy Thompson, assistant sports editor of The Lexington Herald, and Russell Williamson, president of the Kentucky High School Athletic Association.

Films To Be Shown

Honored guests will be the Carr Creek Indians, 1956 Kentucky high school champions to whom the Wasps lost a heartbreaking 68-67 decision in the semi-finals of the State Tournament at Lexington.

Another feature of the evening will be the showing of two films of State Tournament games in which Wayland and its sensational scoring star, Kelly Coleman, participated.

George E. Evans, Jr., who announced plans for the dinner, said it will be an open-house affair, with all Floyd County residents invited. Special invitations have been sent to all county cage coaches and to some in surrounding counties.

Average Over 90

During the past season, Wayland, under Coach Copper John Campbell, won 35 games and lost six and set eight State Tournament scoring records.

The Wasps became the first team in the history of Kentucky high school basketball to average more than 90 points a game. In their 41 games, they tallied 3,709 points for a 90.4-per-game mark —or 2.81 points a minute.

Letters and other awards will be presented to Captain Kelly Coleman, Melvin Robinson, Billy Rae Combs, Billy Fultz, James Hall, Elmon Hall, Curtis Slone, Jackie Thornsberry, Jackie Greathouse and Bobby Bentley, along with the cheer-leaders.

Wayland High, With 86-Point Average, Bids To Become Top Scoring Quint In State's History

By GORDON MOORE, Courier-Journal Correspondent

Prestonsburg, Ky., Jan. 28.—Wayland High School in Floyd County may become the highest scoring team ever in Kentucky prep circles, if the Wasps continue to maintain their present scoring pace.

In the modern-day game, scores and play of the mountain teams stress offense and forget defense altogether in the wintertime sport.

With the scores ranging from 70 to 110 in the majority of games, the emphasis is naturally on offense as it has been for the past four years.

Wayland's Wasps have averaged 86.0 points a game in rolling up 1,893 in 22 outings and have gone over the 80-mark, 3 times; 6 over 90; and 5 times over the 100 mark.

Thus, Wayland scores at the rate of 2.69 points per minute, while the best five leading offensive teams in the United States is from 2.11 points to 2.35 points per minute. Therefore, Wayland scores from .34 to .58 more points per minute than the top five college teams in the country.

In the Wayland-Flat Gap game last Tuesday night, 188 points were pushed through the nets for the highest combined total of 405 games this season and the highest total ever recorded in the mountains. Only last week, Wayland had set a new mark by outlasting Maytown 105-79.

Betsy Layne and Wheelwright had a recent total of 181 points. Other top offensive thrusts have been: Prestonsburg 92, Morgan County 71; Oil Springs 135, Hazel Green Academy 25; Flat Gap 98, Montgomery County 76; Hellier 88, Feds Creek 82; Virgie 89, Jenkins 77; Pikeville 87, Chattroy, West Virginia 78.

Seven teams in the area are averaging more than 70 points a game with Wayland the leader in total points and average.

Defense Becomes Lost Art

Betsy Layne, Feds Creek, Wheelwright, Flat Gap, Prestonsburg and Paintsville trail in that order in total average per game.

Various factors are attributed to the high-scoring with the major one being the great stress on running and shooting. Virtually all high school youths are good shots before they seek a berth on the local cage squad, but very few ever learn to play defense, or even make an effort to do so in a game.

The majority of coaches spend their practice sessions on offensive maneuvers rather than defense, since it is easier work and the results are more gratifying. The cash customers also like to see the ball go through the hoop at a rapid pace.

Individually the picture is the same with Wayland's great shot, Kelly Coleman, soaring to unbelievable heights with each game he plays. He may become the first player ever to score 4,000 points in a four-year high school career. His current 46.5 average is by far the best in the state, if not in the nation and he has nine games plus tournaments yet to play.

Flat Gap's six-foot-five-inch junior center, Charlie Osborne, has a year left and has already averaged 31.1 in his sophomore year and has that rate in 20 games to date this season.

Although a football-playing school that plays only 24 cage games, Prestonsburg has Lowell Hughes, who is flipping them in at a 39.0 point a game pace. A year ago, he was well over 30 for each tilt.

Van Lear's Larry Joe Adams is over the 34 a game mark, and has been in the 25-or more a game class for three previous seasons.

Other top-mountain producers are: Everett Varney, Belfry; Jay Dingus, Warfield; Everett Horn, Inez; Delmar Thompson, Martin; Edgar Rister, Garrett; Homer Osborne and Chet Curry, Wheelwright.

PRESSBOX PICKUPS

By BILLY THOMPSON

Kelly Coleman's Mother Saw Her Famed Son Play Basketball For First Time—On A Film!

The mother of 11 children saw one of her sons play basketball for the first time Thursday night, and she'll probably never forget what she saw. Her son scored 68 points and was given a rousing ovation as he left the floor.

Of course, you may have guessed the player's name since the 68-point total is just as much publicized as the boy himself.

You probably were confused, however, because of his mother seeing him play Thursday night — and you probably saw the game two weeks ago tonight.

You probably did — but his mother didn't.

In fact, she has never seen Kelly Coleman play in person. The only time she has seen him "play" was Thursday night when a film of the Wayland-Bell County game was shown at a big athletic rally at Wayland High School.

Mrs. Coleman didn't go to the games when Kelly played. Friends at Wayland said that Mrs. Coleman "didn't believe" in people putting on "shows and other exhibitions."

Anyway, Mrs. Coleman was mighty impressed with what she saw as she sat with several of her other children at the Wayland rally. Kelly sat at a special table with Wayland Coach Copper John Campbell and the Wasp cheerleaders.

Shively Brown Valentine Howard

Carr Creek, the new Kentucky State champ, was honored guest at Thursday's shindig, one of the few instances that a team which defeated another in the semi-finals being invited to help the defeated team celebrate.

But that's the way they do things in the mountains. There are no hard feelings around Wayland for Carr Creek, which defeated the Wasps by 68-67 on a last-second basket in the semis.

As Campbell said, "Carr Creek and Wayland are double-first cousins. If we couldn't win the State championship, we were hoping that Carr Creek could."

And the Indian chief, Morton Combs, said, "In a chapel program on Monday of State Tournament week, I told the folks, 'Let's hope we win the tournament and Wayland is the third-place victor.' That's the way it turned out."

John Y. Brown, Lexington attorney, made another of his fine talks as one of the many speakers at the banquet. He said, "Let's hope that players from both teams remain in Kentucky to do their college playing."

Of course, he was speaking mainly to Coleman. When Brown made his speech, there had been rumors that King Kelly was going to enroll at either West Virginia University or Kentucky.

After the banquet, I said to Kelly, "Well, have you decided where you are going to play your college ball?"

Kelly turned to me and said, "I appreciate all you have done for me. I would like to come to Lexington, but I am indebted to West Virginia. The folks up there gave me a job during the summer and I can't let them down."

UK Athletic Director Bernie Shively paid the youngster quite a tribute when he called King Kelly the "greatest offensive player I have ever seen."

Here's Reason Mountain Teams Capture Crown—

Since three of the four finalists in the State Tournament hailed from the mountain area (Wayland, Carr Creek and Bell County), many fans wondered the reason. It is easy to see as you drive into the mountain country. I would venture to say that there are at least 50 basketball goals hanging on posts, trees and barns between Stanton and Wayland — that's the reason the mountain teams are good.

Also, you don't see many television aerials rising from the rooftops of houses. You also don't see the youngsters driving around in the family car. You don't see many movie houses or many corner drug stores.

Those reasons, in my opinion, are why the mountains have won the last three State Tournaments.

Shy King Kelly Coleman's Sister Accepts His Award

By Bob Adair

Some 13,000 fans came to hail the "King," but it was a "Queen" who came forward to accept for Kelly Coleman the first of 10 awards presented last night by Russell Williamson, president of the Kentucky High School Athletic Association, to players chosen for the 39th annual all-state tournament team.

Calls for "King Kelly" soon subsided when demure "Queen Linda Carol" Coleman, sister of the illustrious Wayland wonder, took her place at the honor table for the ceremony which included also the presentation of the championship trophy to Carr Creek's Indians for their 72-68 triumph over Henderson's Purple Flash.

Where was "King Kelly"?

"He's kinda shy," explained Linda Carol, and it was evident from her sudden blush that shyness might be a family trait.

"But where is he?" she was asked. "Is he still here?"

The "queen" wasn't sure, but she thought Kelly had gone, avoiding the cheers from Memorial Coliseum, where only an hour before he had raced up and down the court to score 68 record-smashing points in Wayland's similarly astounding 122-89 victory over Bell County for third place in the four-day tournament which attracted more than 100,000 fans.

Finally arrayed at midcourt along with Miss Coleman, a sophomore at Wayland High School, were the following other all-tournament players chosen by votes of coaches, officials and those along press row:

Byron Pinson, Henderson; Pascal Benson, Henderson; Bobby Shepherd, Carr Creek; Harry Todd, Earlington; Corky Withrow, Central City; Dave Eakins, Henderson; E. A. Couch, Carr Creek; Rex Story, Mayfield, and Billy Ray Lickert, Lafayette.

Some disappointment was expressed by fans over the failure of Freddie Maggard of Carr Creek to make the honor list, and probably justly so. Maggard not only was one of the leaders in the championship victory, but in two earlier contests hit winning baskets in the closing seconds of play.

* * *

In addition to trophies presented Carr Creek, Henderson, Wayland and Bell County for first, second, third and fourth places in the 16-team classic, there was a trophy for the cheerleading squad from Shelbyville, voted tops among entries sanctioned by the Kentucky Association of Cheerleaders Sponsors, of which Mrs. Grace Flagstein of the Lafayette faculty is president.

Like Miss Coleman, the five girls who came forward received a [illegible] of whistles from the [illegible].

The Lafayette group was ad[illegible] runner-up, while yell [illegible] Bell County High re[illegible] mention.

[illegible] coach of the [illegible] that win[illegible] provided a bigger thrill than he experienced in 1932 when he sank the winning basket for Hazard against Louisville Male.

Edgar McNabb, president of the Kentucky High School Coaches Association, announced following the final game that Combs will coach the East squad for the association's annual all-star game against the West here next Aug. 11. He will be assisted by John D. Campbell, coach of the Wayland team.

West coaches will be Jimmy Bazell of Allen County and James W. Larmouth of Earlington. Normally, T. L. Plain of Henderson and Jack Story of Mayfield would have been automatic picks, but both were ineligible since they coached the West within the past five years.

* * *

Lafayette's basketball season has ended, of course, but the loss of ace center Billy Ray Lickert still will prove costly to the Generals.

Lickert, whose left wrist was revealed to have been broken during Friday night's double-overtime loss to Bell County, also had been counted upon to be the ace pitcher for Coach Manuel Lyon's diamond crew this spring, just as he was last year.

Donnie Duvall, another Lafayette cager who doubles in baseball, insists that he did not move his pivot foot when he was charged with traveling in the "sudden death" overtime period of the quarter-final thriller.

* * *

It was no surprise to those along press row when Dick Betz of Lexington and George Conley of Ashland were chosen by coaches of the two finalists to officiate the Carr Creek-Henderson title game.

A few of the wise acres quipped that if they were forced to vote, they probably would give the nod to a couple of "write-in" candidates from among the spectators.

Fans finally got to see the two round men of the officiating crew in action together as Travis Combs of Louisville and Milford Wells of Prestonsburg worked the third-place game.

* * *

Keeping up with Kelly Coleman was quite a workout for both men, as well as for the official scorers and others who attempted to keep books on the 68 points. Or was it 69?

Many fans who had booed King Kelly or otherwise criticised his performances in earlier tilts soon were riding the Coleman bandwagon. Even his most severe critics were thirsty for "blood" once Johnny Cox's previous record of 127 points in four games had been topped with 1:43 remaining in the first quarter and soon were screaming encouragement.

Needing only 10 points to equal the four-game mark when the game got under way, Coleman tied it with two free throws after five minutes, 45 seconds of play, looking all the while as unspectacular as usual. The record-breaker came 32 seconds later on the first of two similar tosses, and he also sank the second for his 12th point.

His Majesty the King hit five of eight shots in the first quarter, eight of 19 in the second, six of nine in the third and eight of 18 in the fourth — a total of 27 bulls-eyes out of 52 attempts for a percentage of 51.9.

In addition to the various individual records reaped by the Wayland Wonder, there were countless "unofficial" records posted by the Wayland and Bell County teams.

Besides the separate marks for high score by winning and losing teams, the combined total for two teams in a single game and other obvious new records, some of the "unofficial" ones included:

The separate and combined scores of the Wasps and the Bobcats at the first quarter (34-29), and the half (72-43) and the third quarter (98-65).

Almost overlooked was the fact that three of Coleman's teammates and four members of the Bell County outfit also registered in double figures. Big John Johnson tabbed 32 for the Bobcats despite the handicap of four early fouls.

Many thought King Kelly gave his best rebounding performance in the semi-final game which Carr Creek won, 69-67, considering that there was quite a bit more pressure on him at that time.

One college mentor remarked that he wasn't too impressed by Coleman in games against Shelbyville and Earlington, but that "he convinced me today that he's a great rebounder and a great competitor." After the third-place game, the same coach said, "I'll have to admit that I'm speechless for the first time since I learned to talk."

PRESSBOX PICKUPS

By BILLY THOMPSON

Ole King Coleman was a merry ole netman and as a netman he did thrive.

He dribbled and passed and was seldom outclassed. Tourney record: One-eighty-five.

—Pandit Pundit.

Kelly Coleman, Nearly Exhausted, Returned To Hotel Instead Of Watching Title Tilt —

Many wondered why King Kelly Coleman wasn't around to receive the All-State trophy. His 15-year-old sister, Linda Carol, accepted the award for him as the fans asked, "Where's Kelly?" Linda Carol didn't know, neither did Wayland Coach Copper John Campbell. But when the Wasps got back to the hotel, there was Kelly — just as he had been since the first quarter of the championship game.

"Coach, I hated to run out on all those people, but I was beat. All those kids asking for autographs just about got me," Kelly said.

There is no doubt that Kelly was tired. He told me in the dressing room immediately after the game, "I'm sure glad this thing is over. I am beat."

Kelly went through a lot during the tournament. Hand bills were passed out stating that "King Kelly is in Town, etc." and for a 17-year-old boy from the mountains to be flooded with autograph-seekers, it was more than he could take.

Coleman slipped out of the Coliseum underneath the stands and to the hotel just before the title tilt.

Sports Writers No Longer Will Have To Watch For Records, Coleman Put Marks Out Of Reach —

Wayland's Coleman has come and gone, but the king will reign forever. Perhaps never again will the State Tournament records be felled because King Kelly carried back to Floyd County some amazing marks which left the fans limp as the Dribble Derby came to an end.

Perhaps never again will sports writers and broadcasters have to thumb through the records to weed out individual standouts.

Kelly Coleman Linda Coleman John Campbell Freddie Maggard

Perhaps never again will a player score 68 points in a State Tournament game, or total 185 for four appearances or pitch in 27 field goals in a single outing.

Also, King Kelly's four-game average in the tournament was 46.2 points — which was only .9 of a point from the previous single-game record.

Many fans were so-so about the Wayland warrior until Saturday, but after his two exhibitions in the semi-final and third-place games, perhaps all doubts of his greatness were erased.

Frankly, it is my opinion that he was even greater in scoring 28 points against Carr Creek than in tallying 68 against Bell County. In addition to tallying 28 against the to-be champions, King Kelly hauled in 28 rebounds, got the tipoff at the start of each quarter, did a bang-up job bringing the ball up the court and also passed-off well to his mates.

King Kelly's one desire was putting on a good show — offensively, that is for the fans. Each time he headed into the dressing room after the first three games, Kelly would say, "I'm going to prove to those fans that I can get 60 points in this tournament. They won't be satisfied until I do."

His exhibition against Bell County was a self-satisfying one. The standing ovation given Coleman as he left for a substitute in the waning minutes of the third-place tilt, was the crowd's thanks to King Kelly for a sterling exhibition of basketball.

Coleman is gone, but he'll never be forgotten. The King will live forever in the hearts of those who watched him during the tournament.

Chapter 17

What happened next, after the record setting 68-point game, became one of the most controversial segments of Kelly's life.

Some said Kelly threw on his warm-ups, over his soaking wet uniform, and left Memorial Coliseum, heading who knows where. Some said he showered and then left. Former coach and broadcaster, Jock Sutherland told the Kentucky Educational Television *Great Balls of Fire* documentary that he saw Kelly and his girlfriend sitting up behind him during the championship game between Carr Creek and Henderson.

Kelly says the truth is he's not sure exactly what he did that night. Again he talked to Lexington writer Billy Thompson, still miffed at the reception he had received during the tournament. To add to the confusion, former UK great Wah Wah Jones was quoted as saying Kelly was selfish and overrated and would probably have trouble playing for Rupp at UK. Kelly couldn't believe that Jones, who was from Harlan, would say that about another mountain player. UK Athletic Director Bernie Shively also made a few disparaging comments about Kelly's games. Both Jones and Shively were said to have later been embarrassed by their remarks.

However, one of those in attendance that afternoon was former Kentucky great Frank Ramsey, who had been drafted

by the Boston Celtics but was fulfilling his military obligation at nearby Ft. Knox. Ramsey was impressed, telling
Kelly later that he had heard and read all about him and
that it was all true. He shook Kelly's hand and told him,
"You're great."

For Kelly, emotionally it was to little to late. He told
Thompson that "if these people want to see me play again
they'll have to come to Morgantown." Of course he was referring to Morgantown, West Virginia, the home of West
Virginia University.

Even though Kelly may have watched some of the championship game, one thing is for sure, is that he was not in
Memorial Coliseum when the All-State Tournament team
was announced later.

His younger sister Linda Carol hung around, and when
Kelly's name was announced she walked to mid-court amid
cheers and applause from the sellout crowd expecting and
wondering where the King was. She seemed out of place
standing with the "other" all-staters as flash-bulbs popped
like an electrical storm, recording pictures that would forever become a part of history. Kelly was nowhere to be found.
Fifteen-year old Linda Carol would tell reporters later that
"Kelly is shy."

Almost 50 years later Linda Carol says that certain
memories of that evening in Memorial Coliseum are vivid
while others are hazy.

"I had no idea where Kelly was when they called his
name," she said. "I was sitting in the Wayland crowd just
off of the floor. Someone, I don't remember who, came and
got me and said, 'Linda get out there.' I was painfully shy
then and I would never have done it on my own."

Linda Carol, like many sisters and brothers recalled back
then that Kelly was just a big brother who picked on her
occasionally.

"I never could understand why everyone paid all of that attention to him, " she said. "He was just a big brother to me. Heck, I was only fifteen."

At first Kelly says he went to a downtown Lexington bar with a friend and had a "couple of fishbowls of Michelob." Then he says he went back to the hotel where he ran into Walter Reams, a friend from Wayland. Reams owned a taxi service and restaurant back home, and gambled a little on the side. Over the years quite a bit of his betting success came on Kelly's exploits on the court.

"I ran into him in the lobby," says Kelly, "and he gave me a fifth of Makers Mark. I didn't drink it. I think I gave it to someone on the elevator."

Kelly took great exception to writer Dave Kindred's portrayal of what he did after the game in his book, *Basketball, the Dream Game in Kentucky.*

"Kindred said I went back to the hotel and read comic books," Kelly said years later, still fuming. "Hell, comic books are something you did when you were 11 or 12, not 17 or 18. I don't know where he got that, but it was a lie."

But "stuff" involving NCAA rules would soon be brought into question.

The University of Kentucky wanted Kelly to play basketball in Lexington. Their faithfuls were pressing full speed ahead, in spite of Kelly's announcement he was going to West Virginia. It didn't matter to them. After all, he had not enrolled there yet, so as far as they were concerned, King Kelly was fair game.

Kelly even received a petition delivered to his house in Wayland with 10,000 names on it, all wanting him to come to UK. "I kept it for a long time," he said, "but then it disappeared."

Soon after the state tournament, in late March of 1956, Civic Clubs from Wayland, Lackey and Garrett hosted a banquet at the Wayland gymnasium for not just the Wasps, but Carr Creek's state championship team as well.

There were several speakers that night including Billy Thompson from *Lexington Herald-Leader*, John Y. Brown, Sr., and U of K Athletics Director, Bernie Shively, who said good things about Kelly and wished him well wherever he went to college. Russell Williamson, President of the KHSAA was on hand to make some special presentations to both teams.

Over in the corner that night, sitting in the second row of courtside seats in the Wayland gym was Kelly's special guest, Hubert Kidd, his West Virginia sponsor from Charleston.

It was said that Rupp didn't want Kelly, that he was not a team player, that he lacked discipline. How ridiculous. It was Rupp who called Kelly the greatest player he had ever seen, a combination of several of UK's greatest players. It was Rupp who encouraged former All-Americans Ramsey and Bob Burrow to talk to Kelly, even having their picture made with him, all the time saying good things about the Wildcats.

And it was Rupp who surely must have known that "university representatives" were meeting with Kelly to "work something out."

"Two men came to my school, and we went down to the school cafeteria and they told me they wanted me to go to the University of Kentucky," Kelly offered. "One was John Y. Brown from Lexington and the other was Barkley Sturgill, a lawyer from Prestonsburg."

Brown, who later ran for Kentucky governor and was the father of one-time Governor, John Y. Brown, Jr., was also a lawyer, and a big supporter of Rupp and the Wildcats.

"They said they knew West Virginia had spent a lot of money on me," Kelly continued. "And if I would tell them how much, they would get the money together and repay them and then I would be free to come to Kentucky.

"Heck, I was just a kid. I was under a lot of pressure and they were very convincing, that they just wanted to do the right thing to help me out."

It didn't take Kelly long to figure out he had been duped. But it was too late. "I told them about the car, gasoline credit card, money, clothes, shoes, summer jobs," said Kelly. "Hell, these were two slick talking attorney's and I was just a 17-year-old, falling into their trap. I later resented what they had done, and it helped turn me against UK at the time."

Does it still sound like Rupp wasn't interested in Kelly Coleman?

Adolph Rupp, known far and wide for his over zealous ego, would never allow himself to be upstaged by one of his players, regardless of how good he was. So you could be sure he would maintain an edge over a high school recruit from the mountains - - regardless of how good he was.

"Coach Rupp told me after the Kentucky-Indiana All-Star game that he wasn't sure I could play at Kentucky, wasn't sure I was good enough," Kelly said. "He knew I shouldn't have played at all. He knew I played with the bad ankle. I couldn't believe he used that against me, but he wanted to put me in my place."

Make no mistake about it, Rupp wanted Kelly at UK. There was the time Nat Cooley, the Oldsmobile dealer in Wayland, drove Kelly to met with Coach Rupp at John Y. Brown's home, "just so they could talk about things."

"Coach Rupp told me that he would get my dad a job back home if I'd agree to come and play for him," Kelly recalls. "He said there'd be scholarships for some of my other family and that there would always be a job for me. Heck, I took it to mean I would be taken care of."

Kelly would later say that what West Virginia and Kentucky offered was nothing compared to what other schools promised.

There was pretty much an open invitation for Kelly to come and see the Wildcats play in Memorial Coliseum. Naturally, when Kelly went, there were others who wanted to go, too.

Kelly remembers one trip in particular. It was not for who the Wildcats were playing - - he didn't remember - - but for who went along.

"There was my coach, Copper John; Hoss Halbert, the coach at Martin; Bill Goebel, who coached Prestonsburg; Dog Campbell, the coach at Garrett; Barkley Sturgill, the lawyer from Prestonsburg and myself.

"It was a long trip back in those days, and by the time we got to Winchester, they were all thirsty," Kelly laughed. "We pulled over at a tavern next to the highway. I followed them in and we all sat down at the bar. I wasn't sure what I was supposed to do. Heck, I was thirsty, too. They all ordered beers, and Copper John looked over at me and kind of nodded his head that it was OK for me to do the same. We had a couple of beers and went to the game."

Kentucky had always wanted King Kelly to play for them. There was never any doubt. It's just that Rupp, along with Wah-Wah Jones, UK athletics director Bernie Shively and broadcaster, J.B. Faulconer, were covering their tracks and making excuses in case Kelly didn't come to UK. They could always say, "We didn't want him anyway."

Sure enough, Kelly's dad, Guy, suddenly had a job as a mining inspector back in David, Kentucky, only a short distance from Wayland. It was a good union job that would offer a little more security for Kelly's mom and dad. He moved back from Cleveland, and by all appearances Kelly would be going to UK.

Not so fast."I waited for a few weeks to make sure dad's job was secure and they couldn't take it away from him," Kelly said. "Back then I had so many issues with everything surrounding the school.

"I'm not saying I did the right thing looking back on it, but at the time I thought it was. It all came to an end when Rupp cancelled a speaking engagement in order to meet with me in Lexington. I was told it was one of those meetings where he got paid some money to speak. Anyway, I didn't show up. My dad had a secure job and I didn't want to be bothered with UK anymore. I had to do what I thought was right."

According to Kelly those issues included the fact that UK had caused the NCAA to keep him from playing at West Virginia; and the remarks Wah-Wah made about another mountain boy; and the comments from the school's A.D. And then there was Rupp questioning Kelly's ability and in doing so talking down to him.

If there was one thing Kelly Coleman had other than ability, it was pride. It may not always have served him well, but he had it nevertheless.

There was one other issue that has never gone away, even after almost 50 years. Those boos. He still hears them from the Memorial Coliseum crowd at that 1956 State Tournament. Was it the UK fans way of punishing him because he had chosen West Virginia over Kentucky. Maybe.

So in Kelly's own way he was attempting to even the score.

Kelly and high school sweetheart, Ann Watkins, were married in Wayland not long after the 1956 season ended. It was time for Kelly to make a decision about his future.

Copper John had played college ball at Eastern Kentucky, so he encouraged Kelly to give the Colonels a try. Paul McBrayer was the coach then and he had a reputation for very strict discipline. He welcomed Kelly and for about six weeks Kelly went through a conditioning program and pickup games with his future teammates.

"I wasn't wild about having to do our running through fields that had big holes in them," offered Kelly. "My ankle was still tender and it was easy to turn it again.

"McBrayer was like a drill sergeant. We'd have to line up for inspection. I could handle that," Kelly continued. "But the final blow came one day when he called me in to tell me he was going to change my shot. He said he noticed that I shot it too much toward my right shoulder, that I needed to square it up more. Hell, I told him I had scored over 4,000 points with that shot and I wasn't about to change it now. I was outta there."

Chapter 18

Fred Schaus, who began recruiting Kelly back in 1955, doesn't quite remember the story the way Kelly does. "I never actually saw him play," Schaus says almost 50 years later. "I knew he had a great reputation and he was going to be in the same freshman class with Jerry West. I remember he came up here [to Morgantown] one summer and took some classes or worked. I think he may have even played in a summer league over in Wheeling with Hot Rod [Hundley].

"He was all set to come here and then the NCAA said one of our alumni had given him a gasoline credit card. He was declared ineligible to play for West Virginia and it all amounted to just a slap on the wrist."

Jerry West, considered one of the all-time greats at the college and pro levels, remembered Kelly.

"I remember that he signed with West Virginia," West said some 50 years later. "And then I believe he transferred to another school. I do know he had a reputation as a great scorer."

"Back then the publicity wasn't what it is today - - T.V., radio and all. It's sort of like I lost track of him, but I do recall hearing that he moved around quite a bit. But, hey, I was just a kid myself."

Then West concluded, "People ask me about certain games and players, but sometimes all I can remember is that I played three years at West Virginia and 14 years in the NBA."

It's difficult to believe Schaus didn't know more of the details of Kelly's recruitment. Maybe he didn't see him play. So what, lots of head coaches didn't see recruits play. Perhaps it was just an assistant coach, or possibly he took the word of Elkhorn Coal Company in Wayland.

There were certain things then that a head coach doesn't want to know or need to know. Schaus didn't want to know who paid the $2,000 tuition fee at Greenbrier Military School. He didn't need to know about the summer job Kelly had with the West Virginia Parks system where his job was to shoot baskets, or the apartment he lived in that someone else paid for. Schaus, of course, did know about the gasoline credit card the NCAA turned up. But what about the 1954 blue Dodge with the white top that went with it? Did he also not know Hubert Kidd, who owned a successful insurance agency in Charlestown, West Virginia?

Kidd, was Kelly's "sponsor." He made sure the coal miners son had a car to drive, clothes on his back and in his closet, shoes on his feet, and money in his pocket. That's what "sponsors" did.

"I was dressing like a millionaire's son," Kelly chuckled. "Not a coalminer's."

"Believe it or not at one time I actually had two cars for a while. Earl Clements was running for the U.S. Senate back then, and someone in his campaign committee gave me the car to endorse him. Hell, I couldn't even vote. I'd go home at lunch time and trade cars. I thought it was cool to drive a different car back to school." When Clements lost, Kelly gave the car back.

By Kelly's own admission he went from having nothing to having everything. "I had one pair of shoes to last me for a year, and had to wear my older sisters hand-me-down socks," he said. "Then all of a sudden I had 10 pairs of shoes and all kinds of clothes."

Kelly said there was one occasion where, he, Jerry West and West Virginia football star Sam Huff appeared at a department store promotion in Charleston. "We were served fried chicken and I remember Huff saying he thought it was proper to eat it with your hands," Kelly recalled. "I thought to myself, that's the way I'd always eaten it - - with my hands."

But West Virginia tried to put their own spin to the Kelly Coleman recruiting saga. In mid-July of 1956 they issued a press release stating that they were no longer recruiting Kelly because he only had 15 high school credits. In 1956, practically any school in the country would accept a student with 15 credits. It was West Virginia's excuse. The NCAA investigation had gotten to them.

It would be several months after Kelly had left Wayland, and was working in Cleveland, before Walter Byers of the NCAA office paid him a visit. They talked about more than how the family was doing.

Chapter 19

From 1940 until 1957 Western Kentucky University coaches, Ed Diddle and assistant Ted Hornback, were the coaches from the Kentucky team in annual summer High School All-Star games between Kentucky and Indiana.

Coleman had broken his ankle in a pick-up game in Williamson, West Virginia in May a few weeks before the All-Star game and had been in a cast most of the summer. He had no plans to play in the games in Indianapolis or Louisville.

It would be an understatement to say he was overweight and out of shape. He didn't even plan to dress out.

"Hornback told me to at least be in uniform. The fans had paid to see me," he recalled being told. "Then just before the start, he said he wanted me at least go out for the center jump and after that Coach Diddle would take me out."

Coleman was Kentucky's first official Mr. Basketball and wore number one on his jersey. Some historians say Vernon Hatton of Lexington Lafayette in 1954 and Kenny Kuhn of Louisville Male in 1955 were Mr. Basketballs before Coleman. Oscar Robertson wore number one for the Hoosiers.

King Kelly did in fact feel an obligation to the fans. But he was hurting and did not feel an obligation of doing more than start the game, take a time out and sit down.

"I didn't play much, but probably more than I should," he says. "I barely played in either game and I resent being compared to Oscar Robertson. He was a great player, but I never really had a chance against him."

Coleman recalled that when he went to Indianapolis for the game, there was a lot of hype and publicity for the game. He remembered a luncheon he and the Big O attended. "He ate turkey and drank unsweetened tea, and I had a couple of cheeseburgers and a shake."

Robertson remembers the games and Kelly."As far as I was concerned it was never about me against Kelly," he says. "As for individual matchups, that's not what I was about. It was Indiana against Kentucky as a team."

The Indianapolis game was played at historic Butler Fieldhouse and Robertson remembers back then, in the summer of 1956, it was the hottest ticket in town.

"It was a sellout here and in Kentucky," said Robertson. "It was a real big deal back then."

The Kentucky game site in 1956 was the downtown Armory before moving to Freedom Hall the next year.

Indiana swept both games with Oscar scoring 41 and 34. Kelly scored 17 and 4.

Robertson went on to become one of the games all-time greats at the college and pro-level.

When he finished his three-year career at the University of Cincinnati he is the only player in NCAA history to average a triple double - - points, rebounds and assists.

Robertson went on to be a 1960 Olympian and one of the NBA's greatest with the Cincinnati Royals and Milwaukee Bucks.

He still likes turkey and unsweetened tea.

For the record Kelly was not the first Wayland player to play in the Kentucky-Indiana game. He was preceded by Edd DeCoursey in 1947 and Fred Fraley in 1951.

That summer, all-star games were everywhere. Kelly played in some and others he skipped.

"I was still getting over breaking my ankle in May," he says. "It was really tender, but all of the promoters wanted me to show up. They thought it would help sell tickets.

"There's no way I was close to 100%. I hadn't played for awhile and was out of shape if you know what I mean."

Kelly resented being judged on those games.

That summer there was the three-game East-West series in eastern Kentucky; the Ohio/West Virginia-Kentucky All Star game; the Kentucky-West Virginia game; the Kentucky-Ohio game; the All-American North-South game in Murray; and, of course, the Kentucky-Indiana games in Louisville and Indianapolis.

Chapter 20

How Kelly came to play basketball for Kentucky Wesleyan College in Owensboro fits into his pattern of life; things don't always make sense, but it happens anyway.

He knew quickly that he didn't want to work at ARMCO Steel, a factory in Middletown, Ohio.

"It wasn't something that kept my interest, Kelly says "I fell asleep and it shut down the whole line for quite awhile. It was not a good situation. I realized then I'd rather be playing basketball."

Kelly and Ann had one daughter, Terri Lynn. Kelly left them in Middletown and headed back to Wayland to try and find a school to continue his basketball. Ann was not pleased with Kelly quitting what was considered a good job, so she decided to stay put. "Ann and her family were not at all happy with me," Kelly recalled. "In fact she filed divorce papers there in Ohio."

He began to check around for a school. However, he was building a pretty good resume for failures. For whatever reasons, and there were plenty of them, he had run through West Virginia, Kentucky and Eastern Kentucky, and had yet to play one dribble.

"Dog Campbell, the coach over at Garrett, told me about a coach at Kentucky Wesleyan," Kelly offered. "I didn't even know what town it was in, but I was told they had a coach I'd like to play for."

That coach was Robert "Bullet" Wilson, and when he heard about Kelly Coleman's interest in playing for him, he used all of his old mountain contacts to put in a good word for him.

Bullet Wilson had a long history of coaching players who came from the mountains of eastern Kentucky.He had coached the team, beginning in 1943, when Kentucky Wesleyan was located in Winchester, and many of those team's rosters included players from the mountains. There were those who thought that it took a certain kind of coach to handle the "boys from the mountains."

In 1951 the Methodist College moved its campus from Winchester to Owensboro, and with the move came Bullet Wilson who brought an ambition to build a good "small college" basketball program.

It was common back in those days for a coach to oversee a couple of sports, but at Wesleyan, with budgets being what they were, Bullet coached not only a nationally ranked basketball program, but baseball, golf and tennis as well. And he did it without assistants. There were occasional volunteers, but Bullet was the man in charge.

For the most part Wilson's teams floundered in mediocrity until the 1955-56 season. With wins over Tennessee, TCU, New Mexico and New Mexico State, Utah State, Florida, Western Kentucky, Georgia and Evansville, his team finished 18-4. The four losses came to Washington and Lee, Evansville, and twice to Louisville.

The team did not, however, receive an invitation for postseason play.

A 16-12 record the following year got the Panthers in the NCAAs for the first time ever where they reached the title game, losing to Wheaton 89-65.

So when Wilson first talked to Kelly about enrolling at the 700 student Owensboro college, he could point to a basketball program that was on the rise. They were winners before Kelly.

Kelly liked Bullet, and Bullet liked Kelly. Although he had heard many of the stories about Kelly, he really hadn't had to deal with them up close and personal.

All of that was about to change.

He did know, however, that Kelly had the talent and ability to keep the Panthers in the natural spotlight. Bullet had had a taste of competing for a national championship, and he wanted to do it at least one more time before he retired. Kelly was a player who could give him that chance.

Bullet had a core of supporters for his program, people who were willing to "help out" when needed.

One of those was Fisher Tichenor who owned a Gulf service station on Frederica St. in Owensboro. He told Bullet he would drive to Wayland and pick up Kelly to make sure he found his way to the Wesleyan campus. Kelly had been in this part of the state only once before, and that was for the Central City tournament in December of 1955. It was a long trip, but Tichenor would do it for Bullet.

Tichener had told friends that he had hoped to meet Kelly's family, but that when he arrived at his home in Wayland, Kelly was sitting on the front porch waiting with his one suitcase.

Years later Kelly remembered that he was ready to get out of there when Tichener pulled up in "that big Oldsmobile." "Heck, I went from having two cars to having none," Kelly said, referring to the car West Virginia gave him and the one the Earl Clement's Senate campaign let him drive. He had returned them both.

Rogers Taylor was a senior guard when Kelly arrived in Owensboro, and because he was married, Bullet asked him to take Kelly under his wing. Almost 50 years later Taylor says there is no way his wings were that long."He was his own man," says Taylor. "He was never one for the limelight."

For his basketball talents, Taylor described Kelly as not a great jumper but a great rebounder."When you watched Kelly play he seemed like he was not doing anything," he recalled. "He played so much under control that he made it look easy."

There was one particular game that year that sticks in Taylor's mind. "It was against Louisville in the Sports Center. The Louisville defender was playing Kelly close. Kelly bounced it between the Louisville player's legs, caught it on the other side and laid it in the basket. It was something."

Taylor remembers Coach Wilson telling him during a time out to quit shooting so much."Bullet told me to let Kelly shoot it some," he laughed. "He said that's what the fans had come to see. When we walked back on the floor Kelly took me aside and told me not to worry about it."

Kelly and his wife, Ann, now had two young children, but he was ready to play basketball. That first year the team went 14-10 with wins over Middle Tennessee, Tennessee Tech, Southern Illinois, Murray State, Morehead, Louisville and East Tennessee. Louisville had some pretty fair talent. Among them were John Turner, Bud Olsen and Al Goldstein.

But it was the opening game of the season against Murray State, that caused a little bit of a stir in the Panther locker room before the game. Up until then Murray and Wesleyan had played a total of 13 times beginning in 1935. So what was unusual about this game?

Murray's director of athletics, Roy Stewart, told Bullet Wilson that as far as he was concerned Coleman was an ineligible player because he had enrolled at Eastern Kentucky, an OVC member with Murray State. And, if Coleman played it would be the last year the two schools would play each other. Kelly told Wilson if he didn't get to play he was leaving the team.

"Coach had a dilemma," teammate Don Gish remembered. "But he played Kelly." Kentucky Wesleyan lost that game 80-69 but won the return game in Owensboro 67-65. Murray stood by their word and has not played the Panthers since.

Murray's Terry Darnall remembers playing against Coleman in that last game between the two schools. "I never worked harder at defending a player as I did that night against Kelly," Darnell remembered. "I had heard about him before the season started and just wanted to see what I could hold him to if I really worked."

Kelly scored 30 and Darnell 29.

"He could have been a good defender if he wanted to," Darnell added. "But his game was to score and rebound. And was he rough. He didn't back away from mixing it up with anybody."

Kelly hadn't been in Owensboro long when he received word that his dad, Guy, had been killed in an automobile accident on Highway 7 at Topmost in Knott County, not far from Wayland. He was 51. Kelly grieved. He had a deep seeded desire to please his dad, and now that he had finally settled on a college, he would now be able to make his family proud.

Coach Wilson drove Kelly to Wayland for the funeral.

• • •

Controversy followed Kelly on and off the floor. His demeanor on the court was often overshadowed by the sideshows away from it. Even in college Kelly's life continued to be an adventure.

"I really liked Owensboro and Kentucky Wesleyan," said Kelly. "It was a school where I could play my freshman year and not have to sit out on the freshman team like I would have if I had gone to one of the big schools. We played a major schedule and Coach Wilson said he'd also let me play baseball if I wanted to."

Kelly even told Bullet Wilson about Elmond Hall back in Wayland. Bullet was going to give Hall a scholarship based on Kelly's recommendation. Hall decided to work instead of going to college.

When Kelly moved in the housing unit for married students by himself on the Wesleyan campus, it was like the place would never be the same. Kelly was actually preparing to move into the dorm when Ann called and told Kelly she hoped they could work it out. She dropped the divorce proceeding and Kelly borrowed a car and drove to Middletown and brought his wife and daughter back to Owensboro.

Soon his sister Phyllis moved to Owensboro from Wayland, and with Kelly's contacts she landed a job at Texas Gas. And little sister Linda Carol, the one who accepted his All-State Tournament trophy at the 1956 State Tournament, was a frequent visitor.

Kelly was once again a star. But life was not perfect. He and Ann argued often and when they argued it was loud. Because of the proximity of the houses they lived in, everyone else nearby knew when things weren't going well for the Colemans.

Ann had the children and a job at General Electric. Kelly had his basketball, afternoons and evenings at South Side Bar and Grill, and frequent card games at one of the nearby men's dorms.

Ann knew there were other women. Kelly's charm and star power drew some and he sought others out. There were the notes and phone numbers Ann would find. Often she would call the numbers and confront the women.

"It was Kelly's world and I lived in it," Ann said. "Our high school days were wonderful, sort of like the movie-Grease, sock-hops, riding the bus together to games. It was fun, romantic, but he always did what he wanted.

"Kelly would go to the dorms at night. He said he was playing cards. One time I found money he had hidden in his socks. I got tired of it all, so I packed his suitcase with his name on it and took it over to the dorm and threw it in the lobby. Thirty minutes later he was home."

Then there was the night during a big argument that she threw her wedding ring out in the yard. It took her two hours to find it the next day.

"We had fun, too," Ann added. "With Kelly it was like a story book. We were in love. I just knew things would get better."

Kelly's sophomore year would be Bullet Wilson's last.The 1958-59 team went 14-11 playing a major schedule. The season included two wins over Georgia and Kelly's 25.7 scoring average ranked ninth in the nation. He was also named to the "small college" All-American team, and during that season on December 13, Bullet Wilson fulfilled an earlier promise to Kelly that he would schedule a game in the mountains near Wayland where his fans could see him play. Wesleyan defeated an Eddie Diddle, Jr. coached Middle Tennessee team 77-70 in the dedication game of the Prestonsburg High School Gym. Kelly had 31 points, but apologized for not getting 40.

"I cussed Bullet for years," laughed Eddie Diddle, Jr., years later. "I think we got four or five hundred dollars for playing that game.

"I knew we couldn't guard, Kelly," he said. "So my plan was to guard the other four and let Kelly get his. Hell, I found out we couldn't guard the other four either. I guess the only good thing was we stayed at the Citadel (hotel) in Hazard."

Gus Paris was a history professor at Kentucky Wesleyan during Kelly's years. He also served on the school's athletic committee and therefore had a keener interest in Kelly than perhaps other teachers did. Paris got to know Kelly well. He became somewhat of a counselor to him and in doing so became very familiar with Kelly's personal life - - the good and the bad. "He cost us scheduled games with the big schools, you know the big names," he offered. "Because when Kelly played we beat 'em."

Paris, who later became the school's registrar, has seen most of the great players at Wesleyan, a college that has won eight national championships and appeared in 18 final fours, and he says King Kelly is the best basketball player he's ever seen.

"I asked Kelly what he wanted to do with his life," Paris said. "He told me he wanted to go back to Floyd County and be Sheriff. He said that's the only job he could have and retire a millionaire and nobody would ask any questions."

Paris also had a different perspective on several referees that worked Wesleyan games back then, among them Hickman Duncan.

According to Paris, Duncan loved to come to Owensboro for two reasons - - to eat at Gabes Restaurant and to watch Kelly play.

"Kelly and Duncan would jaw back and forth with a real respect for each other," he recalled. "It added to the game and the fans enjoyed it."

There was another instructor at Wesleyan that remembered Kelly."I had Kelly in class," recalled Dr. Richard Weiss, who now heads up the archives at the school's library. "I didn't know what to expect from him, didn't know if he would be disruptive or what. He was a model student in my class. He participated, came to class and did what was required of him."

"The class was Greek and Roman Civilization and I remember one time in particular that we were discussing the fact that the early Greeks used snakes as part of their worship ceremony. Kelly was sitting there, eyes big as saucers. He came up to me after class and told me there were people back home who did that, too."

Kelly's term paper, according to Dr. Weiss, was Survey of Roman Slavery. "I was very pleased with his paper," remembers the professor.

Bullet Wilson always knew the score on the court and by most accounts knew it off the court, too. He wasn't fooled easily. He'd have to be blind and dumb not to know what Kelly was up to, and he was neither.

Kelly's hang out with his buddies and teammates was South Side Bar and Grill at the edge of town on Hwy. 431, and Bullet knew it. He would sometimes pay a surprise visit.

On one occasion when the coach showed up, they went out the back window and hid in a nearby cornfield. They had to leave so quickly there wasn't time to grab their jackets. Bullet saw them hanging there and decided he'd sit down and order a hamburger. They were shivering in the cold. They got the message.

By the time Kelly's junior year rolled around, he was a marked man. On the road fans booed him, threw things at him and shouted insults, but as the games end neared those same fans would often give him their approval, finally realizing they had seen a great basketball player. Perhaps they had realized it would be a long time, maybe never, before they would see another King Kelly. He had earned their respect.

Bobby Rascoe, who later became an All-American at Western Kentucky and played for the Kentucky Colonels in the old ABA, remembers going to see the King play.

"I was a junior at Daviess County High School and all of the local teams got in free at Wesleyan games," he remembered. "Everyone knew Kelly could shoot, but he was a great passer when he wanted to be. He could handle the ball, and, for his size, what a rebounder."

There were memories of Coleman standing at the water fountain during a time out. While the rest of the team would be huddled, Kelly would be drinking water, lots of water. And then Rascoe recalled seeing Kelly upset after fouling out, going to the dressing room without stopping at the bench, getting dressed and leaving the gym.

Kelly's take on it was, "Why hang around?" "My game and my night was over. What more could I do? The team knew I was for them and where I stood."

One of Kelly's outburst cost him a one game suspension. "Bullet took me out early in one game," he recalled. "I was playing hard and didn't understand, so I went on to the dressing room, showered, dressed and left the gym. Yeah, he kept me out a game. I probably deserved it."

But there was another Coleman memory that sticks in Rascoe's mind.

"A buddy and I were out one night. He knew Kelly's sister who was living in Owensboro. She said a group of people was meeting at Miller Park. We were just in high school so we said let's go. She was sitting between us in the front seat. We get there and she said, 'there's Kelly.' At about the same time someone told Kelly that his sister was over there in the car with two guys. I didn't even know her. . . just along for the ride. Wouldn't you know it, he came over to the passenger side and grabbed me. I thought he was going to pull me through the window. His sister started yelling at him and he let go. Nothing else happened."

T.L. Plain had replaced Bullet Wilson as the coach at Wesleyan, and he inherited a pretty good team. Gary Auten was a guard. He would earn All-NCAA honors and later, in 1961, become an All-American. He was good. Long time Kentucky high school coach, Lyle Dunbar, had spent time overseas in the Army and had never heard of King Kelly until he arrived at Kentucky Wesleyan. Martin Holland, Bill Jackson and Bill Rankin were the tallest players on the team, but 6'2" Winfred Thompson and 6'6" Don Gish were considered two of the teams best rebounders. Gish's 28 rebounds ranked just behind 6'10" Holland's 29 rebounds as the Panthers top two individual performances in a game. The remainder of the 1959-60 team included Allen Wilson (Bullet's son), brothers Bennie and Rob Horrell, Charles Seitz, Danny Grundhoefer, Warren Stephens and Woody Neal.

The Panthers opened the season that year by losing four of their first five games, including a 94-83 loss to St. Joseph's in the Palestra in Philadelphia. That game was the first game of a double header that night. Kentucky beat Temple in the second game.

Wesleyan went on to finish the regular season at 14 and 10 before getting red hot and winning the NCAA regional and advancing to the final four in Evansville.

The Panthers trounced St. Michaels 99-54 in the opening round. But it would be old nemesis and perhaps Wesleyan's biggest rival, Evansville, who would send Kelly and his mates into the consolation game against Cornell the next night.

The 76-69 loss to Evansville was a hard pill for Kelly to swallow, and it would end up being his last game in a Kentucky Wesleyan uniform.

Following the Evansville loss, Kelly and teammate Gish headed out somewhere, anywhere, to drown their disappointment in some spirits. The two ended up in the basement of the Vendom Hotel at a place called the Blues Bar.

Saxophonist Boots Randolph was a regular performer there, but it was the liquor and not the music that drew the pair to this spot.

Kelly told his buddy Gish he was done. He was going to the NBA and that he wasn't even going to play in the consolation game the next day. Gish told Kelly that he would also skip the game. "I went the next day and told Coach Plain I wanted to be released from the team," Gish said. "If I had it to do over I would never have done it. I honestly think that if I had played and insisted on Kelly playing he would have. It was wrong on my part."

Coleman and Gish found another watering hole on the afternoon their teammates were playing Cornell. This time it was a little tavern called the Mecca Bar, then owned by an Evansville horseman named Clem Franks. They spent the afternoon and into the night talking and drinking.

There is this thing about consolation games with Kelly. "I played in my last consolation game back in 1956 at the State Tournament," Kelly recalled telling the press in 1960. "Those games are for the scrubs." Bennie Horrell was the recipient of a starting spot when Kelly decided not to play and those so-called scrubs went on to beat Cornell 86-76 for third place in the national tournament. After the game his teammates knew where they could find him. And they did.

Kelly's decision not to play did not come without a price, however. Even though he and everyone else knew it would be his last game, there were still ways the school and coaching staff could show Kelly their displeasure of his action.

Kelly was considered a lock on an Olympic tryout slot, as well as numerous All-American teams. He had the talent and the stats. Instead of Kelly, Coach Plain made sure Panther guard Gary Auten got the opportunity. "It hurt, but I understood they did what they had to," Kelly said later.

"I was disappointed," says Plain. "As a head coach I had no choice but to suspend Kelly. If I had to do it over again I may have done it a little different."

Plain, over his career, had been an assistant to Rupp at UK, an assistant to John Dromo at Louisville and back to UK where he worked for Joe B. Hall.

"I've been around Westley Unseld, Butch Beard, Dan Issel, and Mike Pratt," Plain says. "Kelly would not have been embarrassed playing against any of them. He had the best finger tip control I've ever seen. He could get more tip-ins."

Plain recalled that Kelly really worked to get in shape at Wesleyan.

"He expected his teammates to play as hard as he did," he added.

It's amazing how much respect Kelly's teammates had for him, even amid some of his antics and actions over his three years at Wesleyan. "He was the best. He could have played in any era," says Don Gish. "He never was as bad as the public's perception. He protected his privacy so much that he cheated himself. His ego and pride got in the way. He was his own worst enemy."

Lyle Dunbar had his own memories of Kelly. "We roomed together on the road," he said. "He was really a shy person in a rebellious sort of way. He liked the attention, but in a crazy way he didn't like it."

According to Dunbar, Kelly was totally committed to his last year. "He wanted the team to really have a good year. I never saw him take a drink during the season."

Dunbar laughs when he recalls trying to set picks so the King could get his shot.

"I'd move over to set a pick and Kelly would yell at me to

get out of the way."Kelly remembers it this way.

"Lyle loved to set picks. Hell, all he would do was bring another defender over to guard me just as I was about to get my shot off. I didn't need a pick."

Dunbar went on to be a very successful high school coach for 33 years in Kentucky, taking Christian County High School to the state championship game twice, so he's seen some talent along the way. "Kelly could shoot and get offensive rebounds like no one I've ever seen," he said.

And what about Kelly's baseball playing days at Wesleyan? Bullet told him he could play baseball if he wanted. This was a sport not played at Wayland High School, but Kelly's love for the game carried over from his pick-up sandlot games on the town's one field.

As ridiculous as it might sound, the King's best sport very well may have been baseball. Wonder what would have happened if he had had the coaching, training and practice? "When I told Coach Wilson that I wanted to play baseball, he asked me if I was any good," Kelly recalled. "I told him I could play in the majors if wanted to." What's the old saying? It ain't bragging if you can do it. And Kelly did it - - even on the baseball field.

Roy Pickerill, Wesleyan Sports Information Director for almost 35 years seemed surprised to learn that Kelly had, indeed, played baseball while there. But after digging through old records he was able to produce some, albeit incomplete records.

The 1958 season stats showed Kelly with a .353 batting average, playing first base and right field. Pickerill's search revealed that on May 8 against Bellarmine, the Panthers won 6-0 and 6-5, with Kelly going 2 for 3 and 2 for 4. On May 13, he went 4 for 8 in splitting a doubleheader with Evansville. He played third base in the second game. And on May 16 playing against Oakland City, he was 3 for 4 in a

13-3 win in the first game and 0 for 3 in an 8-3 loss in the second.

The following year, 1959, very few stats could be found. No final batting averages or anything, except on April 18, doubleheader at Louisville. Wesleyan lost the first game, but won the second 5-3 on a home run by Kelly. Kelly remembered that game. "It was at old Parkway Field," he said. "I hit it so far they're still looking for that ball."

Although many of the old baseball records have been lost over the years, for sure those basketball records weren't.

When the King decided to try his hand at the next level of competition, he had permanently engraved his name in the lores of the Kentucky Wesleyan basketball record book.

Here's what he did:

- Two-time All-American, 1959, 1960
- 1st career scoring average, 27.7 ppg
- 3rd all-time points, 2077
- 1st in points for season, 848, 1960
- 6th all-time rebounds, 904
- 2nd career rebounding average, 12.1
- 3rd in nation in scoring, 30.3 ppg, 1960
- 9th in nation in scoring, 25.7 ppg, 1959

A player's accomplishments should be judged, for the most part, on what he did on every game out. It took Kelly 75 games to score his 2,077 points. Compare that to career points leader Corey Crowder, who scored 2,282 points in 118 games. That's a 19.3 average for Crowder and a 27.7 average for Coleman. If Kelly had played four years and had the benefit of the 3-point goal, it would not even be close. Can you imagine what his point totals would have been?

There have been 10 games in Wesleyan history where a Panther player has scored over 40 points, and Kelly has five of them, with 49 being his highest.

As far as legend-building stories go, Kelly saved one of the best for last. One night after his junior year, he heard someone outside his house. "He was stealing the gas out of my car," Kelly recalled. "I saw him running to the men's dorm and I grabbed my shotgun and went after him."

What happened next was not good for Kelly and his career at Wesleyan. With shot gun in hand he began knocking on doors and lining suspects up. Just as he was checking their hands for the smell of gasoline, a fellow student who was friends with Kelly tried talking him into putting the gun away.

"I wasn't in a very good mood," Kelly would say several years later. "Heck, they were afraid of me anyway, with me being from the mountains, they weren't sure what I'd do, so I fired a shot in the air. Everybody ran."

He never did find the thief.

This episode didn't sit well with the school's administration and Kelly was asked to leave. "Yea, I know I probably shouldn't have done it," he said "But somebody was stealing from me and I took it personally."

He also felt like Wesleyan overreacted to the incident.

"They knew I wouldn't be playing any more basketball so they just wanted me out of there," he says. "Hell, I wasn't going to hurt anybody, just scare them a little."

Perhaps no one had a teammate's perspective on Kelly like Allen Wilson, Bullet's son." He was on the team all three seasons Kelly was there.

Time often wreaks havoc on a person's memories, but in Wilson's case it seems to have given him a chance to reflect on his experience of playing with and watching from the bench as one of the all-time greats played.

"For the most part, I was only around Kelly at practice and the games," Wilson said. "I lived at home and Kelly lived in married housing, but I had a great seat to watch Kelly play."

But what did Bullet say about Kelly when he went home? "Pop never talked about anything Kelly did away from the court," Wilson remembered. "But I do know that he would get upset about Kelly running around. Kelly didn't have a car so he had to get a ride with some of the guys to South Side."

It is a Wilson story that just might hold the answer to Kelly's ability to rebound his own missed shot. Almost everyone who ever saw him play points out that this phase of his game is what they remember most about Kelly.

"I had always heard that Kelly had a goal at his house in Wayland that was on the side of a hill and he didn't want to go down the hill when he missed. He learned to detect which way the ball would bounce and get it before it went down the hill."

Allen Wilson's analysis of Kelly as a player could only come from perhaps a coach's son. "In practice and in a game Kelly didn't expend any unnecessary motion, there was no wasted energy," he says. "He could always play at his pace."

As Wilson looks back, he remembered that Kelly was not a rah-rah guy, not one to try to get the team fired up. At Wesleyan, Kelly was not a big talker on the court.

"He was just a great player," Wilson adds "we ran a motion offense and he just ran the play and when the pass came to him he knew what to do with it. He would shoot it from 30-35 feet but it was in the offense. His shots usually came off the pass, not one-on-one moves."

Wilson says when Kelly first arrived at Wesleyan he was overweight, "maybe 240 pounds," but that he lost it and usually played the entire game. Wilson continues, "He had great hands, but he was not a great jumper. In fact I'm not sure he could dunk. He didn't have to."

Of all the games Allen Wilson saw Kelly play, there are two that really stick out in his mind. "We were playing Evansville and I think Kelly had scored about 40 and played a great game," he offered. "They threw one in at the horn to win. Kelly just fell to the floor. And I'll never forget a game at Tennessee State. Kelly was hitting them from mid-court. Their crowd started yelling for Kelly and he kept hitting."

All of the coaches at Wesleyan who followed Bullet Wilson and T.L. Plain have heard the stories about King Kelly and his days in Owensboro. Who knows how many were true, but according to Kelly there was probably a little truth to all of them.

Mike Pollio, coached there from 1981 thru 1985, and admits that while he didn't know Kelly, he knew the stories about him. "They said there was several times Kelly's teammates or the manager would have to drive out to South Side to get Kelly before a game," Pollio offered.

Wayne Chapman followed Pollio as the head coach, and over his five year span, from 1986-1990, won two national championships. Growing up in Owensboro and playing at Daviess County High School, he's heard them all about King Kelly.

"One of the best ones," Chapman said, "was when Kelly and Bullet were walking across a hotel lobby and several beers fell out of Kelly's duffel bag and rolled across the floor. Bullet grabbed Kelly by the arm and said, "Kelly, let's get out of here, someone's throwing beer cans at us."

Whether it's true or not doesn't matter. It's the fact that someone could tell that story and those that knew Bullet and Kelly knew it could be.

But of all the Wesleyan coaches who knew more about Kelly, only Wilson and Plain, probably knew more than Bob Daniels. Daniels coached the Panthers to two national titles in his five years from 1968-72. However, his first memory of Kelly Coleman dated back to 1953, when

Daniels was a senior all-stater at Oil Springs High School in the mountains, not far from Wayland.

"We were playing Wayland and our coach told us they had a pretty good young player," recalled Daniels." But back then he was just another player. Three years later it was a different story for both. Daniels was an All-Ohio Valley Conference player for Ed Diddle at Western Kentucky and Kelly was on the verge of becoming a basketball legend.

Daniels remembered that in 1956 he went back for the regional finals between Pikeville and Wayland.

"Kelly was unbelievable," he said. "But equally unbelievable was the crowd and all of those people who wanted to see him play. There must have been at least 200 people who couldn't get in."

Daniels had his own theory as to why Kelly was so good at basketball. "It was the eyes. He saw everything. Combine this with great hands and perfect timing and he became special," he added.

Several years later Daniels and Kelly's paths would cross again. While Daniels was coaching the Panthers he encouraged Kelly, living in Wayland at the time, to come back and get his college degree. When he eventually did return to the Owensboro campus, he was welcomed with open arms.

In 1968 he came back with a purpose in his life. Kelly wanted to become a teacher and possibly even coach someday.

His friend, Gus Paris, who by this time was the schools registrar, remembered Kelly's return. "I asked him if he was going to behave," he says. "He said he'd quit all the bad stuff, and he had. He was a model person."

Daniels used to go in the gym and watch some of the pick-up games. "They were the kind where the winners stay and the loser sit," Daniels said. "Kelly's team didn't sit much. Most of the guys didn't even know who he was. And I remember he didn't try to dominate. He mostly set others up with his passing. But, when it came time and his team needed a basket, he'd get it." Don Gish, Kelly's former teammate recounted one game in particular after their Wesleyan playing days were over. "Kelly was playing for Chicago in the ABL and the Harlem Magicians were coming to Henderson to play a game," Gish said. "With me being from Henderson, they asked me to put together a team to play them."

The Magicians were anchored around former Globetrotter stars Goose Tatum, Marcus Haynes and Nat "Sweetwater" Clifton, and like their Trotter days, they expected to win every game.

Gish rounded up a few of his buddies, among them Lyle Dunbar and Bennie Horrell from Wesleyan, and former Henderson player Byron Pinson. They called Kelly, who drove to Henderson from Baltimore to play in the game. In the locker room before the game, Goose Tatum told the thrown-together local team that they should remember their role in the game was to lose. "That was the wrong thing to say to Kelly," laughed Gish. "Kelly told Goose that he didn't drive all that distance to lose, and if the game wasn't going to be played straight he would not play." According to Gish, Tatum further upset Kelly by calling him "kid," but did agree to play the game straight.

Kelly Coleman did his thing, played hard, and scored 33 points, and although Gish didn't remember the final score he remembered that his team did win by seven points, and that near the end of the game Goose was very frustrated. What happened next was somewhat bizarre.

"With less than a minute to go Goose took a round-house swing and decked the referee near center court," Gish said. "I think it knocked him out and as soon as the game was over the Henderson County Sheriff came on the court and arrested him, took him to jail. I know this for a fact because not only was I there, but my dad was the sheriff."

Bennie Horrell remembers how hard Kelly played that night, and looking back on it, after all of these years, how much that game was just one more layer added to the King's legend.

Kelly lets it be known that he enjoyed his days in Owensboro. For the most part Bullet was a lot like his Wayland coach, Copper John. Both would give Kelly just enough freedom so as not to inhibit his spirit or his skills on the hardwood.

Former teammate Gish, marvels 45 years later at how Kelly dealt with the attention he received on and off the court.

"At the beginning of every game Kelly was a marked man," Gish says. "On the road the fans booed him, insulted him, and sometimes even threw things at him, but when it was all over they applauded him. They realized how good he really was." And to further add to the theater that always seemed to be a part of Kelly's life, when it came time to retire Kelly's number he was no where to be found. Don Gish attended the ceremony in Kelly's behalf.

Chapter 21

Kelly could have stayed another year at Kentucky Wesleyan but with his refusal to play in the NCAA championship consolation game, Coach T.L. Plain felt like his only choice was to dismiss him. Perhaps it could have been worked out, but Kelly felt like it was time to move on.He and Ann now had two children, Terri Lynn and Beverly.

In 1960 the National Basketball Association was only an eight-team league and Kelly was drafted by the New York Knicks as the first player in the second round. A simple translation means Kelly was the ninth overall player picked in a group that included Jerry West and Oscar Robertson.

Red Holtzman signed Kelly to a Knicks contract with a $2,000 signing bonus. There was even another $2,000 for Kelly if he showed up for the first practice under a certain weight. He didn't collect it.

Carl Braun was the Knicks coach, and from the very outset Kelly got off on the wrong foot with the coach and the team's star player, Richie Guren. "I didn't have one of those guaranteed, no-cut contracts," Kelly says. "And it wasn't long before I got myself in trouble."

According to Kelly, he and Guren had several on-court confrontations that carried over to their social hour. And by now Kelly was almost as big into social hours as he was basketball. His beverage of choice was anything with alcohol in it.

It didn't take long for word to travel to the other seven NBA teams that the Knicks had a troublemaker on their hands. It seemed Kelly Coleman, the rookie from Kentucky Wesleyan, was difficult to coach.

As much of a party boy that Kelly had become, he was still a talent on the court. But one night while enjoying himself while out with the guys at a local club, in a drunken stupor, Kelly tripped and fell down a half a-flight of stairs, cutting his head. The final roster cut was only a couple days away and this incident was what made the Knicks decision to release Kelly an easy one.

"My reputation was bad, drinking, partying and all," said Kelly as his eyes teared up. "I was considered not worth the trouble. It was my own fault."

And almost 50 years later Kelly still believes he was better than over half of the players in the NBA. "I know it and they knew it," he said.

Kelly weighed his options. His children, Terri Lynn and Beverly, were back home in Wayland with Ann. He still knew he could play at the game's highest level. He also knew he was responsible for his own actions. He still had something to prove, but he would have to do it in the old Eastern Industrial League. He signed on with Baltimore where another Kentucky legend, Bill Spivey, was his teammate.

"There were some great players in the league," Kelly offered. "Many of the guys had gotten in trouble with gamblers in college and the NBA didn't want them. This was the only place they could play."

It wasn't long before Kelly was out of Baltimore. Abe Saperstein, who also owned the Globetrotters, started the

American Basketball League and signed Kelly to a guaranteed contract with the Chicago Majors.

Manny Jackson and Governor Vaughn were on the team, and so was 6'11" Ken Peterson, who knew of Kelly from his collegiate days when Kelly was at Wesleyan and Peterson at Murray State. "He was such a clutch player," recalled Peterson. "When we needed a score he could get it.

"I knew about his reputation. He could party all night and never miss a beat the next night. What a legend he was," Peterson added.

The ABL folded after only two seasons. Kelly's last season saw him lead the league in 3-point baskets, to the surprise of no one who had seen him play at Wayland and Kentucky Wesleyan. He ranked as the ABL's number three scorer and in the top ten in rebounding.He knew for sure he would be picked up by the NBA.

It was not to be.

Harry Gallatin, a NBA all-time great, who had seen Kelly up close and personal while coaching at Southern Illinois against Wesleyan, told the King he was done in the NBA and that he should move on.

"It hurt, It really hurt me," says Kelly. "I saw players that were not even close to my ability being picked up by NBA teams. My reputation was still out there."

Donnis Butcher, another great mountain high school player from Meade Memorial and Pikeville College, had played against Kelly back home. He knew all about him. Butcher spent a year with the Knicks during the 1960-61 season. He saw Kelly's demise but there was nothing he could do. Butcher's claim to fame as a player came during that year with the Knicks when he played in the game against the Philadelphia Warriors and Wilt Chamberlain. The game was played in Hershey, PA. That night Wilt scored an NBA record 100 points.

Soon after, Butcher was traded to the Detroit Pistons where he played, and later became head coach. "Kelly was a great basketball player, who for several reasons never made it," Butcher said.

Kelly played hard and partied hard. It had become his life style. "I never had any proof, but someone had to really put out some bad information on me, because no one wanted to even give me a chance," he said.

After the ABL disbanded, Kelly was somewhat forced to play for teams that played against Saperstein's Trotters. He didn't like it and lasted for a half a season. Along the way he became friends with Sweetwater Clifton, a former Globetrotter and NBA star.

Kelly recalled a trip to Harlem with Clifton. "Wilt Chamberlain owned a bar there, and Sweetwater asked me to go with him," Kelly said. "Wilt was sitting on a bar stool when we went in. He asked me who I was and I told him I was Kelly Coleman, the guy who had broken his high school scoring records. He laughed, we shook hands and partied a little bit."

Kelly was 25 years old and by this time he and Ann had three children, son Kelly had recently been born.

Professional basketball was over for the King.

Chapter 22

Kelly, Ann and the three kids decided they would get a new start on life and move to Cleveland. Kelly had two sisters living there and two other sisters lived in Akron. It looked like the Coleman family had now done what so many other coalmining families from eastern Kentucky had done over the last decade - - moved to Ohio to find work.

He hired on at Republic Steel and Ann found work with Western Union. Kelly didn't like his job. He had had a taste of factory life before and he knew this wouldn't last long. For the most part Ann liked her job, with the exception of singing Happy Birthday over the phone.

"We had been there a few years," Kelly says. "And at this point in my life I was thinking I need to get my degree."

All the while, Kelly's younger brother, Phillip had been a promising basketball player at Wayland in 1963. It was not easy following Kelly, but nevertheless the 6' 1" Coleman was good enough to receive some college offers, among them Furman. College, however, was not in his future, and eventually Uncle Sam came calling.

The Vietnam War was raging and if you weren't in college, Vietnam is where you usually landed. Phillip went to Vietnam, and in late October of 1966 the Coleman family received the dreaded knock at their door in Wayland. Phillip had been killed. He was 21 years old.

Kelly and Ann added a fourth child, Mary Ann, and reality had set in that he needed to get beyond his basketball past. He was several credit hours short of his college diploma.

The Coleman family headed back to Kentucky, back to Wayland.

Kelly leased a service station in town from the Elkhorn Coal Company, and at almost the same time enrolled in two classes at nearby Pikeville College.

It didn't take long for word to get around the small campus that King Kelly Coleman was a student there. One of those who heard that Kelly was around was Steve Butcher, who was the nephew of Donnis Butcher. Steve was active in intramural basketball, and his team, made up of some of the local good ole boys, was in the finals. Their opponent was another group of students who hailed from New York and New Jersey. "It was the championship game and I asked Kelly if he would play for us," Butcher recalled. "He said he'd come by the gym and if we needed him he might play."

Butcher wasn't sure Kelly would give it another thought. He didn't think he'd show up. After all, Kelly hadn't played in a while, was out of shape, and overweight. Why in the world would King Kelly Coleman show up at a Pikeville College intramural basketball game? Because, he loved to play.

Sure enough there he was, shooting warm-up shots. He was ready.

All of these years later Butcher still can't believe what he saw.

I'm not exaggerating," Butcher says. "He hit 10 straight three-point shots. We had a 17-point lead. Kelly asked if that was enough, and grabbed his coat and left the gym. All of us stood there in amazement."

With the encouragement of Bullet Wilson, Gus Paris and basketball coach Bob Daniels, Kelly went back to Owensboro and enrolled at Kentucky Wesleyan.

"They really did me a favor to let me come back," says Kelly. "I was a model student. I'd go to class during the week and drive home on weekends."

In the spring of 1968 Kelly Coleman got his college degree, and after an unsuccessful run for state representative, he sold his lease in the service station and once again he and Ann, and their four children, headed north, this time to Lincoln Park, Michigan, where Kelly had a teaching job at Lincoln Park High School. He was a teacher, not a coach. "I'm not sure what kind of coach I'd have been," he said. "Maybe I would have expected too much. Who knows?"

Kelly enjoyed teaching, but didn't like the salary. One day, after two years at the high school, he answered an ad seeking someone in the circulation department at the *Detroit News*. Ann had already been working there in the advertising department for almost two years.

Kelly says the paper had the largest afternoon circulation of any paper in the United States, and paid him three times more money than he was making as a physical education teacher.

Not only was the money better for Kelly and Ann, but he won a trip to London, England that first year by achieving certain goals. He felt good about himself.

He and Ann seemed to have their life in order. Kelly had quit drinking, and although Ann's dream had been to have that little house with the white picket fence, she was relatively happy.

Kelly took another job when, in 1976, he bought a service station in Monroe, a town between Detroit and Toledo. Business was good. He owned three wreckers, one being one of those oversized haulers that specialized in semi-tractor trailers on the nearby interstate. "I was making money." Kelly said. "But then the gasoline shortage hit, and then when the shortage ended, the dealer owned stations began to really undercut the little independent owners like me. Hell, I was working two jobs, couldn't sleep, and actually lost weight." He sold the station in 1980.

Still working at the *Detroit News*, he bought the 37-room Gaylord Motor Inn in 1989. It was located on I-75 and business was good enough that a year later, he left his job with the newspaper after 20 years. Ann was still there and Kelly spent most of his time fooling with the motel and dabbling in the stock market.

Kelly's mom, Rusha, had been the family's rock. At the age of 78 she was still going strong. However, in 1992 she died from a heart attack. The loss was tough on all of the Coleman family. After all, in the early days it was Rusha who kept it all together while Guy was working in Cleveland.

In 1994 he sold the Gaylord Motor Inn.

"I retired," he said. "I just decided I'm not working anymore. I had played the market a little, made some good investments, and made some money on the sale of the motel."

For several years things had not been particularly good between Kelly and Ann. The kids were grown and money didn't seem to be a problem. But they were having difficulty. On the surface you would think they had the rough part of their lives behind them. But it was not the case.

In the winter of 1997 Kelly went to Florida, and when he returned to Michigan things weren't any better. It was then that he decided he was moving back to Wayland.

He moved into the house that his mom and dad had bought a couple of years after he had gotten out of high school. It was in total disrepair, needing new electrical, plumbing, and roofing. "You name it and it needed it," says Kelly.

It was 1999, and in September of that year Kelly and Ann, after 43 years of marriage, divorced.

The basketball hero who went by the nickname of King Kelly, and the pretty majorette who had been called Queen Ann had called it quits.

For years their relationship had not been the fairy tale they had hoped for. Ann had been the stabilizing factor in the family while raising the four kids and working full-time. Kelly, in his mind was trying his best, becoming the best provider he could be.

In the early years it was his drinking and other women. As they worked through crisis after crisis within themselves, all the time still in love with each other, in the end that love was not enough to keep them together. Their differences, known only to them, was too much to overcome.

Ann described Kelly as "that old racehorse who wants to feel the wind in his face one more time."

Over the years Kelly had developed a fondness for golf and fishing. It was not something he could readily do in Wayland, but there was a place called Woodson Bend, near Somerset, Kentucky. It offered golf and fishing on Lake Cumberland. He thought he would try it out and in October of 1999 he rented a condo there.

Two months later he was back in Wayland.

He had heard about a place near Crossville, Tennessee, called Fairfield Glade. The golf was great and the fishing was good. He drove down and soon after bought a house there.

He was there a year, when one day he was notified that club member's green fees would be increased from $19 to $35.00. Kelly, being Kelly, didn't like it. "I said no way. I went to the realtor the next day and put my house up for sale."

It was January 2001 and in April his home sold, and he was back in Wayland.

"I really didn't want to leave Tennessee," he says. "I liked the area and the people and I had heard about Lake Tansi Village Resort." Kelly bought a home there in February of 2002. He could walk to the club house, and he could have his fishing boat in the lake in a matter of minutes.

Life was good. He had everything he wanted. Golf, fishing, and one of the best things of all, people didn't know who he was. In a way the King was trying to hide from his past, not telling his golfing buddies that he was King Kelly Coleman, the greatest high school basketball legend in the history of Kentucky basketball. Not telling them he scored 75 points in one game and 68 in a state tournament game.

Not telling them that he had been booed by a capacity crowd because he was the best. Not telling them that he had been a college All-American.

He talked basketball with them and had his favorites in the NCAA Tournament that March, but that was all they needed to know. His life was his business and nobody elses.

"One day there was a knock on my door," Kelly laughed. "This guy says that he had seen me several times at the clubhouse and wanted to know if I didn't use to play basketball somewhere. I told him I had played at Kentucky Wesleyan. He said, 'I thought so,' and turned around and left."

For years Kelly had suffered from back pain. In November of 2003, when the pain became almost unbearable, he went to Middletown, Ohio for back surgery.

"It was bad," he says. "There was a pinched nerve and it affected my left foot. I couldn't live with it any longer."

Kelly spent four weeks in recovery staying with his daughter Mary Ann. But for Kelly it suddenly looked like the roof of life was caving in. An eye problem developed. He became concerned about going blind. He then self diagnosed himself with cancer. "I thought this was the end," he says. "I put my house up for sale in Tennessee and moved back to Wayland." Kelly had drawn up a new will and bought a cemetery plot at Davison Memorial Gardens where his mother, father and brother Phillip are buried. "I thought I was dying," he said.

KELLY COLEMAN, 6'3" Small-College All-America forward, Wayland, Ky.
KENTUCKY WESLEYAN COLLEGE

"Married housing" where Kelly and Ann lived

Kelly, daughters Terrie Lynn and Beverly, wife Ann. In the background Ted Hombock (left) and Ed Diddle

Kelly with his West Virginia University "sponsor," Herbert Kidd of Charleston, WVA. Kelly was recovering from a broken ankle sustained in a pick-up game in Williamsburg, West Virginia.

Kelly in his practice uniform at Kentucky Wesleyan

Laying one in at Kentucky Wesleyan

"King" Kelly Coleman

Kelly and wife Ann in their Kentucky Wesleyan days, daughter Terrie Lynn sits on Kelly's shoulders while Beverly is on his knee

KWC Coach "Bullet" Wilson

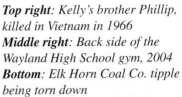

Top right: Kelly's brother Phillip, killed in Vietnam in 1966
Middle right: Back side of the Wayland High School gym, 2004
Bottom: Elk Horn Coal Co. tipple being torn down

Wayland H.S., 2004

Wayland H.S. gym, 2004

Kelly inside the Wayland gym, 2004

Wayland, Kentucky, 2004

Kelly inside the Wayland gym, 2004

The modern Wayland Community Center/Historical Society

Bobby Hamilton's Wayland Kwik Mart in 2004

South Side Bar as it appeared a few years after Kelly left Owensboro

Kelly and Wayland Kwik Mart owner Bobby Hamilton in front of a group of Kelly's photos

Curtis Ray Slone cuts Kelly's hair in Wayland. Slone was a freshman on the 1956 team with Kelly

Rusha Coleman

Kelly with granddaughter Courtney

Carr Creek Coach Morton Combs

King Kelly Coleman Highway

Kelly Coleman, 2004

Chapter 23

In 1988 the Kentucky High School Athletic Association inaugurated its Hall of Fame. Missing from that first group of inductees was Kelly Coleman. It did not sit well with him. He felt that his credentials as a high school basketball player in Kentucky took a back seat to no one, and his exclusion upset him.

The following year Kelly's name was at the top of the list.

"Thanks but no thanks," Kelly told the KHSAA. "If they didn't think I deserved to go in the year before, I sure as hell wasn't going in then.

"Some of their people gave me all kinds of excuses why I was initially excluded. One person told me the second induction ceremony was going to be in Lexington, and not Louisville like the first one, and that it would be easier for my family to get to Lexington. It was like my family couldn't find their way to Louisville. Then someone else said they wanted to save me for the second class so it would draw a big crowd. I didn't buy that either."

There were a couple of other underlying reasons for Kelly's refusal.

He had never really gotten over fellow mountain boy Wah-Wah Jones' remarks about him when he played at Wayland. And when Jones went into the Hall of Fame's initial class, that only added fuel to the fire.

"Wah Wah couldn't carry my tennis shoes when it comes to basketball," Kelly would say.

Kelly, now digging for more reasons as to why he turned the KHSAA Hall of Fame honor, points out Dawahare's, the clothing store, sponsorship of the Hall of Fame. It was their strong support of Pikeville back in 1956 that still lingers. But then he says Dawahare's outfitted him with clothes when he played in some all-star games following his senior year. And finally there's his belief that his high school coach, Copper John Campbell deserves inclusion in the Hall of Fame. He says "local mountain politics" has kept this old coach out while others with lesser credentials have gotten in.

Copper John coached for a couple of more years after that 1956 season, and his son, John Anthony, is not sure his dad ever really got over that one point loss to Carr Creek.

At one time the Wayland coach had aspirations of landing a college job, perhaps as assistant at Kentucky or Eastern, but then he decided to do what his father and grandfather had done. . .go into the retail merchandising business. He took over his dad's store. He ran the store until he died in 1977 at age 56.

Kelly pretty much has an open invitation to accept induction into the Hall of Fame. Julian Tackett, the assistant commissioner of the KHSAA says, "We'd love for Kelly to agree to be inducted. He left such a mark on high school basketball. The fans love him and I would hope that he recognizes that."

That love from the fans was further emphasized in 2001 at the Boys State Tournament in Rupp Arena, when the Kentucky High School Association of Basketball Coaches invited the best 50 state tournament players of all-time to make an appearance. The great ones were there, but it was Kelly who brought the house down.

"I was standing next to him when they introduced him recalled Tackett." It was unbelievable. It was emotional. They loved Richie Farmer and Rex Chapman, but when Kelly Coleman was introduced the crowd went crazy."

Chapter 24

Kelly wasn't dying after all. His self-diagnosis was wrong. His doctor told him he didn't have cancer. The eye problem was controllable and the back would get better.

The scare caused Kelly to rethink his life a bit. He's opening up, becoming more visible, and even, after all these years, becoming more comfortable with who he is. And even what he has become - - a basketball legend. Adults want his autograph. Fathers who saw him play and fathers who didn't want their sons to know about him.

One man told sports columnist Bob Watkins that he had lived a good life. He'd seen the three kings: Petty, Elvis and Coleman.

"There was so much pressure on him growing up," says Rebecca Hall Hohn, the former Wasps cheerleader. "He stayed away from Wayland all those years, I think partly because he felt like he let the town down when he didn't become that great pro basketball player. But he didn't let anybody down, maybe only himself."

Kelly Coleman now accepts it. He knows the good and the bad better than anyone else. He has experienced incredible success and failures. He can look in a mirror and know who to blame and who not to blame.

For the most part those boos from Memorial Coliseum in March of 1956 no longer echo in his mind. They have been replaced with handshakes from admirers who probably never saw him play, but have only heard the stories about the legend.

"I just went through a period in my life where every decision I made was the wrong one," he says. "If I should have gone left, I went right, and when I should have gone right, I went left.

"You know, I did a terrible job of growing up, but I think I've done a good job of growing old."

Today, the canvas where Kelly performed the art of playing basketball, the wooden Wayland gym, still stands. It is ironic that another King now owns it. David King bought it a few years back, along with the high school building built in 1941 that sits adjacent to it, and rents it by the hour to those who want to shoot hoops on the same court that the real king did.

At the end of the gym, up on the wall behind the basket, hangs an aging sign. Though faded over time, it serves as a reminder, to those who followed, just what the Wayland Wasps and their star player, accomplished in that 1956 season. The sign list the names of the players, coach, managers and cheerleaders and was dedicated by the Kiwanis Clubs of Prestonsburg and Martin.

• • •

In hindsight it probably wasn't fair. These basketball players, all across Kentucky, their faces not yet wrinkled by time, were too young to have to carry such a burden. The hopes and dreams of entire towns were loaded on their shoulders. Some never recovered.

Kelly remembered when he was in his old coach Copper John Campbell's health class back at Wayland High School. Copper John leaned back in his chair spinning one of his many stories to the class, nothing to do with health or school. Suddenly the door would swing open as school principal Lawrence Price walked in unannounced. Without missing a beat or even looking around, Copper John would say, "And that's the way the heart works."

Perhaps the final chapter has yet to be written about Kelly Coleman. One can only wonder what might have happened if he had not scuffled with his fellow cadets at Greenbrier Military Academy, and refused to take orders from upperclassmen. Then he would have missed the 1956 State Tournament, never to be mentioned in the tournament record book. Oh yes, he would have still probably been a special player, but not the legend he became.

If that had happened the state of Kentucky would have been deprived of seeing, reading and hearing about the most legendary high school basketball player to ever play in the state. Forever, King Kelly Coleman and Wayland will be linked. The two names are almost interchangeable. You don't say one without thinking of the other.

His place in basketball folklore is set in stone, and King Kelly Coleman is, indeed, Kentucky's greatest basketball legend.

Kentucky High School (KHSAA) Records

Team Records – Wayland High School
Most Points per Game (avg.) – Season 91.0 (3rd)
Most Free Throw Attempts – Game .... 93 (1st v. Pikeville, March, 1956)
State Tournament Team Records – Wayland High School
Points – Half .... 72 (1st v. Bell County, 1956)
Points – Quarter .... 38 (1st v. Bell County, 1956)
.... 34 (3rd v. Shelbyville, 1956)
Points – Both Teams .... 211 (1st Wayland 122, Bell County 89, 1956)
Points – Tournament 341 (2nd, 1956)
Field Goals – Game .... 48 (2nd v. Bell County, 1956)
Field Goals – Tournament .... 137 (2nd v. Bell County, 1956)
Individual Records – Kelly Coleman
Most Points – Career 4,337 (1st 1953-56)
Most points – Season 1,734 (1st 1956)
Most points – Game .... 75 (6th v. Maytown, 1956)
.... 68 (12th v. Bell County, 1956)
Most Points per Game (avg.) – Season 46.8 (3rd 1955-56)
Most Points – Half ....39 (5th v. Pikeville, 1956)
.... 39 (5th v. Henderson, 1956)
.... 38 (6th v. Bell County, 1956)
.... 33 (8th v. Wheelright, 1956)
Most Field Goals Made – Game .... 27 (3rd v. Bell County, 1956)
Most Rebounds – Game .... 41 (2nd v. Maytown, 1956)
State Tournament Individual Records – Kelly Coleman
Most Points – Game .... 68 (1st v. Bell County, 1956)
Most Points – Tournament 185 (1st)
Most Points – All Tournaments 185 (7th*)
Field Goals – Game 27 (1st)
.... 16 (7th)
Field Goals – Half 14 (1st)
.... 13 (2nd)
Field Goals – Tournament 69 (1st)
Field Goals – All Tournaments 69 (7th*)
Free Throws – Game 18 (2nd)
Free Throws – Tournament 47 (1st)
Free Throws – All Tournament 47 (4th*)
Rebounds – Game .... 28 (1st v. Carr Creek, 1956)

only played one tournament

National High School Records
Most Points – Career .... 4,337(7th All-time)
Most Points per Game (avg.) – Season (1956) .... 46.8 (10th All-time)

Out Takes

(Observations by the author as he researched the book)

1. Sitting with Kelly and watching an old 16mm video of the Wayland vs. Earlington game was something special.
2. Shooting baskets with Kelly in the Wayland gym.
3. Trying to understand how Kelly could score so many points in such a short period of time.
4. Marveling, after reading reams of newspaper articles, at how Kelly could deliver such point productions with all that pressure on him. He was the ultimate example of a marked man. Every coach and every player wanted to stop him.
5. Seeing the tears in his eyes and the emotion in his voice as he explained the bad choices he made in his life. Kelly once told me. "If a person ever tells you he wouldn't change a thing in his life, he's lying."
6. "You can write anything about me you want to," Kelly told me. "As long as it's the truth."
7. "Honestly, there's some things I can't remember, it's been almost 50 years," he said.
8. Jerry Fultz of the Wayland Historical Society, who helped immensely with the book, and whose brother Billy was on the 1956 team, was a pretty good player himself. Graduating in 1967, he once scored 49 points in a game.
9. There's something about the name "King" in Wayland.

David King now owns the old Wayland gym and high school, and Jerry Fultz's wife's first name is King.

10. Murray State coach Rex Alexander said he liked Kelly's game a lot, although his shot selection wasn't the best. He reasoned that he would probably score no more than 20 points against a strong defensive team like Mayfield High School. Which quarter?

11. Copper John Campbell of Wayland and John "Dog" Campbell of Garrett are cousins.

12. Kelly spent much of his time during timeouts drinking water.

13. Proof that time can play tricks on the mind: Kelly said that over time he had convinced himself that the game winning shot Maggard hit against Wayland was from 30-35 feet. Elmond Hall has convinced himself that the shot was "slung the length of the floor." The shot was actually 22-23 feet.

14. Knott County, one of the state's least populated counties, produced state champion Carr Creek in 1956. Also, four of Wayland's players were from Knott.

15. The most frequent name I ran across in doing the book was "Hall." The Hall name was everywhere. Not even a game program helped.

16. The most commonly misspelled names I encountered was E-L-M-O-N-D, not E-L-M-O-N, as in Elmond Hall; and F-R-E-D-D-I-E, not F-R-E-D-D-Y, as in Freddie Maggard.

17. I spent a total of seven days in Wayland on three separate visits. Three nights were spent in a charming cottage managed by the Historical Society, next to their office.

18. When Kelly came back to Wayland after graduating from Kentucky Wesleyan, he told some of the younger kids that it was probably not a good idea to chew gum while you played basketball. It could throw your shot off a bit, he said.

19. Kelly was named as Floyd County's Youth Chairman for the "Earle Clements for Senator" campaign. Kelly was only 17 when named to the post but assured the committees that he would register and vote.

20. Guy Strong, the well-known high school and college coach, never saw Kelly play but heard that he once showed up at halftime of the Wayland at Wheelwright game wearing a bathrobe. Kelly says it was a long overcoat and he had his uniform under it, ready to play the second half.

21. I'll never forget sitting in legendary Carr Creek's Morton Combs' home with Kelly and Jerry Fultz talking basketball.

22. Make no mistake about it; the Historical Society/Community Center is the biggest building in Wayland. It is safe to say that it has the town's only elevator.

23. Kelly is not pleased with the way the town looks. "It didn't use to look like this," he said.

24. Kelly is still very much a celebrity at the annual "Wayland Reunion." Men and women bring their children and grandchildren by to get Kelly's autograph.

25. When Kelly's brother, Keith, found out I was doing the book he wanted to make sure I got "all of the good stuff on Kelly."

26. It seemed like everyone interviewed for this book has a King Kelly story, even if they had never met him or seen him play.

27. The enjoyment I got in hearing and seeing Kelly open up as the development of the book progressed was very satisfying. It seemed to be like therapy for him.

28. Elkhorn Coal Company was originally spelled Elk Horn.

29. Kelly hasn't had a drink in 17 years.

30. Kelly's birthday is September 21, 1938.

About the Author

Gary P. West grew up in Elizabethtown, Kentucky and attended Western Kentucky University before graduating from the University of Kentucky with a degree in journalism in 1967.

At UK he was a daily sports editor for the *Kentucky Kernel*.

Later he served as editor for the nation's largest civilian enterprise military newspaper at Fort Bragg, North Carolina. From there he went to work for one of the country's largest insurance companies as a copywriter in the corporate office of State Farm Insurance in Bloomington, Illinois.

In 1972 he returned to Kentucky where he began publishing an advertising shopper in Bowling Green.

Along the way, for twelve years, he worked in the athletic department as executive director of the Hilltopper Athletic Foundation at Western Kentucky University, and provided color commentary for sportscaster Wes Strader on the Hilltopper Basketball Network.

In 1993 he became the executive director of Bowling Green Area Convention and Visitors Bureau.

He is a freelance magazine writer in addition to writing a syndicated newspaper column, *Out & About...Kentucky Style*, for a number of papers across the state.

Gary P. West

Index